My Son, My Daughter

by Adejoke Oludayomi

xulon PRESS

Dedication

To Abba Father

The Best Parent Ever

Acknowledgements

I wouldn't have had much to say in this book if it wasn't for the memorable years that I spent as a daughter to Chief Adetona and Chief (Mrs) Eunice Bosede Balogun, my parents. I want to say thank you for all you have been to me, my siblings, my husband and my children. The way I am now, is because of the way you were then. Forever grateful.

Huge thanks go also to my children, Tosho, Tobi, Timi and Tise for letting me write about you and those beautiful years when God allowed me to be your mother. Though I say I can't wait for you all to "Fly the Nest", you know I'll miss you terribly.

Olubunmi, my beautiful new daughter in law – thank you for choosing to become a part of our lives. You know we love you so much already.

I'm especially grateful to all the young people who shared their heart felt feelings about their lives and their growing up years and have allowed me include them in this book. Seyi Daniel Ajao, Paris Asakome, Oredola Smith, Maxine Johnson, Renee Audifferen, Lola Olukogbon, Nancy Nwaka, and Jesunifemi (which actually means Jesus loves me) Ogbonmide. I really appreciate your contributions.

Special thanks also to my friend, Dr Mrs Idowu Osibodu and all the dear women who shared their experiences about bringing up their daughters with me, because before now, I didn't have any.

A big thanks to all the staff of Xulon Press. Your encouragement and support has been wonderful.

And to 'Niyide, my first and only love. Thank you for twenty seven years of parenting with me. Without you I wouldn't have been able to write this book.

My Son, my Daughter
By Adejoke Oludayomi

Contents   Pages

Prologue

In the Beginning...

*I*t's July the 8th 1986. I'm shivering, shaking and trembling all at once. One part of me, the dignified part is whispering into my ear, "Sssh. Get a grip on yourself. It's nothing new. People are watching."

The other part of me, a part I never knew existed is forcing me to let out a blood curling scream.

Was that me? I never knew I could scream that loud. And who cares who is listening. All I want is for it to be all over. The months of waiting and joyful expectancy have vanished in the last few hours. Right now, I'm only thinking of myself.

"Get out! Get out!" I find myself frantically pushing at the foreign body that is causing me so much pain.

Okay I've had enough of you. For months you have eaten my food, taken up all my space, following me around, every where I go, you're there. Wearing my clothes, sleeping on my bed. These days I don't even have enough room to stretch out comfortably on the sofa and though I have tolerated you with some what expectation these past months, today, the party is definitely over. ""Out you go."

"One more push", the man standing at the foot of the bed coaxes. Just one more. You're almost there, almost there."

One last push. One final yell and something shoots out of my body. So fast the man at the foot of the bed has to make a quick save and catches it or should I say catches "him", just before he falls to the floor.

"It's a boy!!! You have a baby boy!" they yell.

Yes, there is more than one of them in the room. Three to be precise. Two nurses gathering round and the doctor struggling to keep hold of a slippery, blue (yes – don't ask me how or why but bright blue) new baby boy. 3 people all looking at me in my not so dignified position. Not that I care.

I'm totally exhausted now but the feeling of exhilaration is welling up inside .

"Why on earth is he blue?" I'm wondering and crying at the same time.

I'm also musing at the young man jumping up and down, actually almost somersaulting right outside the hospital room door. I'm thinking, "Good for you, at least you have the strength and power for that. I can barely think."

Slowly but surely, I come out of the daze and my pulverized body begins to relax and calm down.

My husband is in the room now, gazing in wonder at his "not so blue now, but not yet completely brown" new baby son. The baby is yelling at the top of his voice and I am ...still crying...for joy.

As much as I can remember, that's a short account of the arrival into this world of Omotosho Ayodeji Onaopepo Fadayomi as he was named then. Try and pronounce it. The names have changed over the years. Now, if you meet him he'll introduce himself as Tosho or you may even get away with calling him Tosh. First born, first son. The first of four. All mine. All so very different.

For little did I know then, that I would be going through that experience 3 more times. In different circumstances and places over the next 8 years. And learning so much as the years roll by.

A bit of which I want to share with you. You'll probably see yourself and your experiences mirrored in mine. Or you may learn some precious lessons you can tuck away for the future, you never know.

But right now, I'm the newest mother on earth, enjoying the feeling that comes with bringing a new life into the world. And feeling so very much blessed.

Chapter One

Needs and Wants

You see it every now and then in the supermarkets.

Crying child, usually about 2 to 5 years old, either whining, grumpy, complaining, crying or down right rolling on the floor in the middle of the aisle. Why? Wants something off the shelf that mummy isn't getting for him.

It could be little boy already has something like it and doesn't need another one.

Or it could be little boy's friends at nursery have it and he wants it too.

Or it could be that mummy just plain cannot afford it.

Summation of the story, little boy isn't getting it.

Full stop.

Even if you are a multi millionaire, there will be sometimes when you will have to say to your child, "No, you just can't have it".

Sometimes it hurts you yourself because you know your child's heart is set on it. But it just has to be no.

Children need to realise as early as life as possible that they can't have everything they want.

So even if you are a multi millionaire, there are things that even you cannot buy. Like the presidency of the United States or captain of your schools football team.

Your child needs to know from the very beginning that, that is life. Money cannot buy you everything.

There was a king in the Big Book[1] called Solomon[2]. He was slated to be the wisest and richest king of his time. He had everything. Seven hundred wives and three hundred mistresses![3] If he wanted he could have had a different woman every night for almost two and a half years. (Must have been so tiring though!)

Whatever his eyes saw he had to have it. And they destroyed him eventually. Not that he died young or anything, but he lost the zest and excitement of pursuits of life. He became disillusioned. And He lost his relationship with His Creator.

"Meaningless! Meaningless!" he cried. "Life is so Meaningless."

"What is new?" he cries. "I have seen it all".[4]

"Well not exactly Solomon," I quietly reply. "I bet you haven't seen a plane or a micro wave or even an IPAD. You couldn't have. They weren't even invented in your time. Unless you had a vision".

Why had life become so unexciting for him? He had everything. Anything he wanted, he had to have it. He got his people to pay enormous taxes, to fuel his lavish extravagant life style.

By the time he was ready to move on to the next life, they were fed up of him and made sure they let his succeeding son know.[5]

We need to teach our children that they can't have every thing they want. Of course there is a difference between a "want" and a "need". We need to decipher between the two.

It's the end of the school year for your 16 year old and to make it the school has a ball room dance to send them off to the next stage of the lives. Your teenager will need something nice to wear that evening. True. He needs to look his best. True. Do you need to break the bank account because of that? No! Especially when it'll be lying under the pile of unworn, un-ironed clothes in the laundry room for the next 6 months.

So when he or she (most likely it'll be the "she") starts cajoling and pleading for that sensational priceless dress that will knock every one breathless and knock you even further down the debt ladder in the process, you've just got to say "NO!".

Like I said earlier, money cannot buy you everything. Even God will not give you everything you want.

Everything you need – yes – but not every thing you want.[6] He has promised to supply all your needs because he has the riches to do so, but He hasn't said you or I can have just about anything.

One of the reasons why this is so, I think, is that we need to discipline ourselves and tell ourselves that even though this is beautiful to look upon we will not allow ourselves to have it.

Discipline is one of the virtues of greatness.

We discipline ourselves when we decide not to have that piece of cake, even though we are dying to have it.

We discipline ourselves when we decide to fast and abstain for food for a while.

We discipline ourselves when we wake up early to pray or set time aside to do a load of iron or house cleaning.

Does God give us our "wants"? Sometimes, yes. The Big Book says the desires of the good man will be granted.[7] So if you are considered good in God's sight, He promises to give you what you want or desire. But there is a small catch there. Your desires must be in line with God's will and what He feels is good for you.

And that should be the same principle we use with our children.

They may want something that we may think may not necessarily be a need in their lives, but we decide to give it to them anyway. Why?

Sometimes it's because we can afford to.

Or it could be because they have been good and we'd like to reward them.

At other times it may be because it might just do them some good to have it.

The underlying rule should be – do they need it or do they just want it?

If they need it, then we try as much as we can to get it for them.

Do they just want it? If we think it would be good for them and we want to give them a treat, then they can have it.

The lesson is, it's best to teach them early enough that life will not give them everything they want. And neither will you.

So whether it's a tuxedo for the school prom that'll cost you £1,000.00 or the ball room dress that may cost even more, sometimes you've just got to say, "Sweetie, I'm sorry you just can't have it.

Take it or leave it, baby. All the whining and sulking is not going to make me change my mind."

Chapter Two

Just Because They Liked it Yesterday...

*I*t's Thursday evening and after a long day at work, we are slowly, tiredly trudging down the aisles of our local ASDA[1] store.

We decided that Thursday was the most convenient and economical day to shop for the house.

First of all because the store isn't as full on Thursday as it is on a Saturday morning

Secondly because it's closer to the weekend than the first 3 working days of the week and hopefully the groceries will last until Saturday afternoon.

I say "hopefully", because the children are up very late on Friday night, and a whole weeks shopping seems to fade away with the night just as Saturday morning dawns.

I don't suppose you've ever heard this phrase from your kids, "There's nothing to eat in this house, mom", even though the cupboards were full of cakes, biscuits, sweets, bread etc just 24 hours before.

Maybe we should put some locks on the cupboard doors...

Anyway, it's Thursday again and the my husband Niyi and and I, are again in ASDA carrying out our weekly shopping chore.

Cheerios, Cornflakes, Rice Krispies, Weetabix are all staring down at us from the cereal aisles on either side.

"Now what do we buy today?" he says out loud.

"It's Weetabix, they want" I reply.

"Are you sure?" he asks.

"Positive!"

2 Packs of Weetabix find some space amongst the other groceries fighting for room in the trolley.

Milk, sugar, bread, squash, ice cream, bagels, you name it, it finds its way into the trolley... The list is endless. No wonder we can't keep our weight down.

Finally we find our way to the check out and eventually after denting our bank balance by about fifty pounds we drive slowly out of the car park.

The thing about children is that they change their minds about what they like or don't like as often as day turns over to night.

You'll discover that there'll come a time when you either keep the receipts of the clothes, shoes and bags you buy for them or you just give them the money for what they need and let them go out and get their stuff themselves.

21

When they are old enough that is. You just can't keep up with their changing tastes in everything – food and groceries inclusive.

"Hello, everyone", I yell as I come through the front door. "Is anyone home? We're back!"

"Hi mom," my youngest son shouts back from the sitting room, where he's sprawled in front of the TV at the same time playing some football game on his laptop.

He does that so skilfully, you wonder if he can cook a sachet of noodles and wash the dishes at the same time.

I certainly can.

You mentally stiffen the nag about the electric bill for this month.

"I could do with some help unpacking these groceries", I yell back.

Everything comes tumbling out – sweets, chocolates, milk, apples, biscuits on and on and on, until ...

"Mum! Weetabix! Why did you buy Weetabix?"

"Err... I thought you liked them. You asked me to buy them". I reply.

"Told you," my husband mutter under his breath.

"Mum, that was last month.... just because we liked them then, doesn't mean we'll like them forever. We've had enough of them for now... Prefer Cheerios ".

"Okay", I reply, " next week, Cheerios, it is. But I'm not returning the Weetabix. Just make sure that they are all finished before then".

Hubby and I make a mental note, next week ...it's Cheerios

It's just that next week, like tomorrow never comes ....

Chapter Three

Sibling Rivalry

"Mom, I don't like Tise," Timi whispers in my ear.

I burst out laughing. Real loud.

All my sons names start with T. Timi is the third in line to the throne and Tise (pronounce Tishay) is the last of the lot.

It's Sunday. Service is over and everyone's gone home. Pastor's family is left packing up the electrical appliances safely away in the storage cupboard, allocated to us by the landlord church. Not having bought a place of our own yet. we rent their hall for our Sunday afternoon services.

Still laughing I walk up to the rest of the "royal family." Tobi, second son and Tise are busy hoisting our loud speakers on to the shelves in the storage cupboard.

"Guess what? Timi said he doesn't like Tise" I announce.

Everyone, including Tise, burst out laughing.

Of course it was just a joke but we know the two of them have their squirms and disagreements more often than not.

When you have 4 children, even though people say they look alike, they have very different personalities and so there's bound to be some friction between them.

Thankfully the oldest, who is also the quietest, is four years older than the second, and so the gap between them makes for a healthy relationship.

The next three are two to two and a half years apart and so the bulk of the conflict occurs between them.

"You are always on Tise's side" the two in the middle say.

"You're always picking on him", I reply.

"He's selfish. Never shares what he has with us and yet he's always wearing our stuff. Never takes permission. Never asks us first".

They have a point there. He's in sixth form so he wakes up earlier than they do, to go to school. They work very late into the early hours of the morning running their business, so they sleep late. He's able to sneak out of the house, wearing their stuff.

What do you do when your children seem to be always at each other's throats?

You are torn between one and the other. You don't want to and you must not, show favouritism to any one child above the other. Sometimes they both have a point – they may both be right in the circumstances (if you are married I presume you'll realise that this is very possible). However as soon as you try to mediate between them they still think you are taking sides.

There's a woman in the Big Book who had this common problem. Her children were confrontational to each other right from when they were in her womb. They were a set of twin boys and the younger held on to the heel of the older even as they were being born.[1] Talk of trying to be physical even at that age! The Big Book doesn't tell us how their childhood panned out but by the time they were adults you could see that a lot of scheming and jealousy was in place. Their mother, Rebecca preferred the younger son and must have shown it as the years passed by.

Her husband Isaac preferred the elder one. This might have been because he seemed to be the more physically rugged of the two, and definitely because he liked to eat the savoury meat that the older son brought in from the wild.

The story talks of two incidents in their lives that had a negative effect on their relationship.

According to Jewish law the first born son of a family was entitled to twice the portion of the inheritance of their father when he passed on to the next life. So even though the brothers were twins, Esau was born first and so was to inherit two thirds of their dad's possessions. Jacob was to get one third. Each brother knew what was coming to him. It was Jewish law and they would have known it at their Bar Mitzvah[2], probably at the age of 13.

But one day Jacob voices out his desire to have what was by birth, Esau's. He bargains with a very hungry Esau and exchanges a meal of pottage with the right to be the first born.[3]

Stupid of Esau really as he was home already and there must have been something he could nibble on in the house to stave his hunger but there it is. Either he must have been quite gullible to have agreed to the exchange or maybe he thought, "no witnesses, no written down exchange on paper. Nobody is going to believe Jacob anyway".

The second incident occurs some time later. Dad is very old and getting ready to die. He wants to bless his sons but lo and behold he seems to have only one blessing to give and that must go to the first born. So he asks Esau, his first born, to tickle his fancy, prepare him a delicious meal so that he can be motivated to pour out this huge blessing on him.[4]

Now we know that technically, Esau isn't really his first born anymore, because he sold his birth right for some measly pottage. But old daddy Isaac doesn't know that, does he?

Now we need to understand the scenario and the cultural practices of that time. The fathers blessing was considered to be very important and potent in those days.

A fathers blessing or curse, as it may well be, was able to make or break a son or daughter in life. It is still the same today, anywhere in the world. When a good father blesses his children, they will definitely and surely be blessed. But a curse can have terrible repercussions in the future of a son or daughter.

Anyway to cut a long story short with the help of his mom, Rebecca, Jacob succeeds in deceiving his father, Isaac into blessing him with the blessing that should have gone to his older brother Esau. (Or should it have?)

The entire story is written in the book of Genesis, the first book in the Big Book.[5] It's an interesting story that you'll enjoy reading in full.

Esau is devastated when he eventually finds out and the sibling rivalry that must have been in existence all these years escalates into a death threat. "Dad will die soon and then I will kill my brother", he vows.

Sibling rivalry if not properly managed by both parents can lead to anger, hatred, family splits and possible murder eventually.

Jacob has to run for his life. He lives in exile for 21 years. By the time he returns his father, miraculously is still alive but so very old, denied of his second son's presence for so long. His mother is no longer mentioned, so we presume that she has died.

What a high price to pay by both parents for not managing the relationship between their two children properly.

Do they sort it out in the end?

Yes they do but after so much heartache and needless suffering.

Most families with more than one child probably experienced some form of sibling rivalry. I remember my older brother, 'Seinde on one warring side whilst my younger brother, Femi and I were on the other. With eight and eleven years between me and my younger sister 'Funke and the "baby" 'Jide respectively, there was not much friction amongst us. But they had their years of skirmishes and disagreements too.

If your children are always fighting amongst themselves weigh the situations. A little rivalry is okay, it prepares them for the outside world. It's a jungle out there and they must be ready for competition. As long as the show of brotherly sisterly love is evident at other times, all is well. Some siblings seem to fight like cats and dogs at home but would stick up for their siblings and tear any adversary to pieces when they are both outside the home. A kind of unwritten pact , "No one bullies or beats up my brother (or sister), but me".

But as a good parent, keep your eyes and ears open and be ready to mediate fairly and justly between them when the need arises. Remember both you and them will be the better off for it, in the end.

"Tise!" I yell. "Why are you wearing Timi's trainers without his permission? Mind yourself oh! (a colloquial way of saying you behave yourself or watch it!!) "

He smiles at me when he sees the twinkle in my eye.

I'll call it "Sibling Mediation Strategy (SMS)". You may call it "Peace making".

Whatever you call it, you need to devise yours.

Shalom!

Chapter Four

To Smack or Not to Smack

As far back as I can remember, in the sixties and seventies, in most families, you misbehaved, you got walloped. That means you were sent to get a branch off one of the surrounding trees or hedges in the back garden yourself and you were quite painfully then taught the lesson of not lying, not stealing, not doing your homework, not learning your times table on time, etc. etc. etc.

I remember once, I must have been about 9 years old then, I climbed on top of the boys quarters roof to retrieve a number of black boards my grandmother had confiscated from me one sunny day. I was actually playing with my dolls and had "built" them a house with the black boards that were normally used to teach us some extra lessons at home after school.

For some reason that was supposed to be for "my good", my paternal grandmother (God rest her soul), decided to spoil my blissful recreation time and got some of the young men who lived with us to place them right out of my reach, on top of the back house roof. We called the back house, a bungalow of 3 or 4 rooms, the boy's quarters.

I must have been devastated, and she must have underestimated the boyish determination in me. I scaled the walls of the building, climbed on to the roof and brought the boards down.

In her eyes it must have been the worst thing I could have ever done. As soon as my dad got back from work, she told him how I put my life in danger or at least my neck ... by climbing the Mount Everest walls and retrieving the boards, when she had expressly told me not to.

Have you ever heard the remark, "This will hurt me more than it hurts you?" We know that that isn't really true, don't we?

It's usually said just before a very angry parent wallops you for some misdemeanour you have committed.

Whilst trembling in fearful anticipation of what is about to befall you, you are thinking, "if it hurts you so much then, why not let us change places".

Well, I got walloped for climbing on top of the roof and can still remember the lesson until today. Never climb another wall again. And honestly I'd have to be chased by a hungry roaring lion, these days, to be motivated to scale any roof or wall. When you weigh ten times heavier than you did then, you'll understand why. Anyway I learnt that lesson so very well.

Well, that was over forty years ago and times have changed. It's a new world now so I decided to ask a couple of younger people. Young men and women in the late teens or early twenties. What did they think of smacking?

Oredola is an undergraduate in Keele University in Staffordshire in the United Kingdom.

"Sometimes, in my home, we regarded as annoying, the way we were disciplined as children, but we were kids and didn't really know or understand that much" she acknowledges.

Grown now, I have realized, that firm discipline was very much necessary as I could have ended up – on the fast lane – in a bad way. I might have found myself stuck in a situation or rut that we see many a young adult in now . Looking at how their lives have panned out, I do feel sorry for them, but maybe a more disciplined upbringing may have made a world of difference in their lives."

She reminisces, "There are times when your parents may restrain you from doing certain things and they'll say to you, "when you have your own kids, you will understand what I am doing" or "when you grow up you'll see why I am doing this".

And she admits that as children we may not really understand what lies behind the decisions parents take to ensure their children are brought up properly, when we are younger, or how useful they will be for us when we grow up.

Oredola is at that stage where she thinks maybe she should have a firmer understanding of the reasons behind the firm family discipline in which she was brought up, by now, but sometimes she just doesn't understand.

"I guess the day is coming, I suppose, when I will have a fuller realization of things and say to myself, "ohhhhhhkay. . . I seee why now"".

Yeah, I agree with you, Oredola. Probably when your brood are driving you up the wall.

I remember there was quite a good measure of smacking or physical punishment in our days. We dreaded it so much that, we found ourselves being good, not particularly because we wanted to but because of the fear of the consequences that could follow. You threw yourself into your school work at boarding school because you knew if you didn't you would get into trouble at home. You didn't sneak out of boarding school without permission because you feared your dad more than what the school authorities would do to you in the event of you getting caught.

Did we fear our dad then? Yes, we did.

Did we love him regardless? Yes we did.

Did he love us, provide for us, buy us clothes, toys, books – anything we needed, send us on holidays abroad? Yes he did.

Did we enjoy the smacking, caning then? No we didn't.

Did we all – the 5 of us – three sons and two daughters – turn out to be well adjusted adults, balanced, happily married parents of our own children? Yes, we did.

Would we use the same methods of discipline bringing up our own children? Maybe with not the same tenacity and maybe with different methods but we would still have the same reasons and the same objectives in mind.

When if at all do you smack a child?

The Big Manual tells us that if we spare the rod (cane, stick, hand on the bum) we will spoil the child[1]. Spoil the child means that the child will not grow up to be what God created him/her to be. Such a child **may** go astray. Note the emphasis on the word **"may"**.

A child or even an adult may err or do something wrong, for 2 broad reasons.

One reason could be that the child (or adult) is ignorant of what is right.

The Big Book Manual says where there is no law there is no wrong doing.[2] If there is no knowledge that what we are doing is wrong, then it would be unfair to be punished for doing it. However we know that in today's world ignorance of the law will not safe you in a court of law.

A child may not know that it's wrong to hit another child or he may not know it's wrong to take something that belongs to someone else. The Adamic nature in man (and woman) means we will naturally do what is wrong. We will not naturally choose to do what is right. We need to be told or taught what is right from what is wrong. Some of us learn quite quickly. Some of us don't.

For instance, you are your dad and mom's little 2 year old son and they warn you, " Our friends are coming over with their little 2 year old son, this afternoon. Be a good boy. Be nice to him and don't bite!!!!".

But despite the warning, you bite him the first time and you get told off. I mean, you're barely 2 years old and biting feels good. It kind of eases the feeling of irritability in your milk teeth. Never mind the screams of pain coming from the object of your assault. It feels good to you.

So little toddling baby Jide is told off, actually screamed at by his parents and has some daggers of looks coming from the visiting parents. They say "It's okay. He didn't mean any harm. Don't spank him". They say it with their lips but their eyes are warning you, "If you do that again, we'll thump you!!"

First error. Little boy is ignorant of the consequences and effects of his action.

Does he do it again?

Twice, before they leave. And the little visiting baby John, is clinging to his parents now, so fearful of those weapons of mass destruction hidden discretely away in your mouth.

Has baby Jide learnt a lesson? No.

Does he need a little help learning it? Yes!

A little smack on the back of the hand will help in learning the lesson quicker, I should think. I have heard of instances long ago, where a little bite on the hand, teaches the lesson even faster. The lesson was, this is how a bite hurts, so don't do it to someone else.

Not now! I wouldn't advise you do that in this age or the Social Services would be knocking at your door.

The second broad reason why a child or an adult would err is when they are aware of what is right, have been told of what is wrong but go ahead and do it anyway. This is called wilful disobedience. You have been told (and you must be told, before you can commit this offence) not to do it, but you do it anyway.

So what does that tell us parents and those who are in authority over children?

Children must be told what is right. The Big Book Manual says, "Train up a child in the way he should go and when he or she is old they'll not stray off the way they have been taught to walk on".[3] Some children are soft hearted and willing to walk the right way with minimum training, teaching or cajoling. Others are more defiant and strong willed and will need a bit more pressure and discipline. You will not kill a child when you smack or spank or will you?

Child Abuse

What is child abuse and when do you draw the line between correcting a child and abusing him?

Any type of discipline verbal or physical that leaves a mark on the body or the soul of a child is abuse.

Child abuse is a sin against the child, his God and the law and is punishable by the laws of the land, at least in the UK.

But the law does not say a child cannot be spanked.[5]

Even when a child is being spanked he or she must be aware that you love him. He must know why he is being disciplined and must be drawn back to you when the discipline is over. A child must not be afraid of you, he must be afraid of the punishment. He must know what to expect from you when he does anything wrong. He must know the difference between a punishment for not doing his homework to pushing another child in the ditch.

If you smack a child for every little mistake, you are a tyrant because you are not perfect yourself. How would you like God to whack you over the head every time you did something wrong? If your child goes about with a downcast look and is not free to be himself in the home, your mode of discipline is very wrong. Your child must know once the punishment is over, all is forgiven and your love for him is as strong as ever.

When do you stop smacking?

Some children rarely need a spanking. A sharp glance in their direction does the trick. Some may need to be shouted at before they do what is right. However there are the unfortunate few, (I hope) who may need a hand on the hand or bum once in a while. It is hoped that by the time a child reaches the age of reasoning, which differs from child to child or even sibling to sibling, you will not need to smack any longer. And definitely not any more when they have reached puberty. How can you spank a girl who has become a "little woman". Other forms of discipline should be in place long before then.

A friend of mine whom we will call Jayne remembers how it was when she was growing up in her teenage years.

There was the feeling of rebellion when you got to that so called "I'm grown up age" and you don't want to do any chores around the house. Don't boss me about. I'm a woman now". But like we all learnt, rebellion got you nowhere. Back then you did what you were told to do or you'll be punished.

In those days, the entire community were involved in bringing up a child. You dare not sneak out to forbidden night parties for fear of being seen by someone who knew your parents. And if you were misbehaving in public be sure to know that your mom would somehow find out about it. Pheeewww!

Those were the days when bringing up a child was relatively easier, I would say. Not any more. Everybody minds their own business these days.

Pity.

As Jayne would say, growing up back then was quite good. We look back at the discipline and upbringing that our parents put us through and marvel. We didn't like it then and wondered why there were all the rules and regulations. But now? We're grateful for that kind of upbringing.

Raising your child with words

Nancy tells us how most of her Nigerian friends find it strange when she says her parents never beat her.

"My siblings and I were raised with words" she says.

"They raised my four siblings and myself to understand the full consequences of our actions".

"As a kid, however, I would sometimes wish that they had beaten me. The words they had with me left the weight of the world on my shoulders. Even though I felt it's pros and cons, the heavy talk made me become responsible at a very young age. I applaud my parents because without having to beat us they were able to instil a sense of "Corporate family responsibility" in us. We understood how our individual actions reflected and impacted on the family as a whole. We are therefore driven to achieve our best in what we do set out to do - academics and all. Why? Because our achievements make everyone proud."

"Because I've seen my parents putting the needs my siblings and I, first and foremost, before theirs, I understand that when they do discipline us it's definitely for our own good. I'm proud of my family and hope to be able to do both the discipline and love for my children, when I have them".

But back to our question now, what do you think?

To smack or not to smack?

With the love of God and the love of your child, rooted firmly in the back of your mind, you decide.

Chapter Five

No You Can't!!!

"*B*ut Mom, everyone's going to be there." She wines. "You never let me go any where. I miss out on all the fun. I'm never going to get married if I don't go out, you know. I'll be an old maid".

"Yeah sure", you muse, inwardly of course. "You're not even 13 yet. It'll be a long time before you become an old maid, sweetie".

"Mom?" she's cajoling now." Please, let me go". "They'll be talking about it at school next Monday and I'll be the only one who wasn't there".

Why does she always ask for permission to do what she knows inside of her that I will not let her do? When I was her age I never even bothered to ask because I knew they'd say no. Why does she always try?

"Well...Ask and it shall be given to you," a quiet Voice inside reminds you. "If you don't ask, you don't get".

"Yeah, but she's asking amiss" you reply.

"How do you know she's asking amiss?",the Voice in your head asks.

"Well, it's an 18 year old's party and they'll be guys way older than her there."

"Correct, but his 13 year old sister is your daughter's friend and she'll be there".

"There'll be alcohol and getting drunk".

"Maybe, maybe not. Have you checked".

"Well, no...".

"Maybe it'll be better to make a few phone calls. The family is listed in the phone book".

Find out the full facts

Bringing up children can be a daunting experience, especially in this age of the internet, Apps, mobile phones etc . You try to keep up with the changing world of technology as much as you can but as soon as you understand one mobile phone another new type comes out. And frankly you really can't be bothered to keep up with all the changes.

But you have to be careful that just because your dad and mom forbade you certain things when you were growing up, doesn't necessarily mean that those things will be bad for the next generation.

Think about mobile phones. You probably had your first one when you were almost 30. Now children are having them as early as 8. It doesn't mean your child has to have one that early but you need to keep up with the needs of a different generation. A generation so widely different from yours

So before you rely on your preconceived traditional intellectual mindset, ask a few questions.

An hour and one telephone call later you know so much more than you did before and can make an informed decision which probably may not be "no" after all.

Yes, it's an eighteenth birthday party

Yes, there'll be older boys there

Yes, his younger sister is your daughter's best friend

You also find out after speaking to his mother....(surprised he has a mother!!), that it's really a family type of party – all ages will be there. Moms and dads, children, nieces and nephews, uncles and aunties.

You also find out that the birthday boy is a keen sports person who although currently in his first year in Uni[2] comes around to his former school to help take the year 8[3] students in volley ball and has invited some members of his volley ball class. And guess who is also in that class? Your daughter. And who is head of Sports ? His mother! (Head of Sports – a woman? Oh well!)

Party starts at 4 pm because it's a Sunday and they'll have been to church in the morning. You also find out that it ends at 11pm because it's half term holiday and there's no school the next day and they DON'T DRINK ALCOHOL!

Underage children are to be dropped off and picked up by their parents. Parents will be required to register their phone numbers at drop off point.

"Sue!!" you call and watch her brooding face light up when you say, "I've thought about it and have decided that if dad's okay with letting you go, you can".

Of course, you're not going to let on that you checked it out, she'll find that out in due course. You know dad will let her go any way. He'll let her jump off a cliff if she didn't intervene.

"Oh Mom! She screams giving you a tight bear hug! "I do love you!"

" I love you too, my love," you say, relieved that it went well… (thank God) …………… this time.

Next time it may have to be a definite no.

When it' has to be a "no" ………..

Sometimes, a lot of times, you'll have to say "no" to your child or teenager. You know as well as I do that they need protection from the evils of this world and they hardly ever see as far ahead as you do.

In the Big book there's the story of a girl, probably a teenager of about 16 who had a bit too much freedom in a strange land her family were travelling through. She was left on her own to go sight seeing and just as it happens today she fell into wrong company and got raped. The Book doesn't say she was a bad girl.

44

She was just in the wrong place at the time without the proper supervision that was required for her at that age. The young man who defiled her, fell in love with her and wanted her hand in marriage, but the act was a dishonour to both her and her family at that time. It led to a wide scale bloody vengeful assault on the boy and his family and many lives were thereby lost.[4]

So when your teenager asks and you have to say no for her own safety or for some other reason, when she asks "Why?" don't say,

"Because I say so!"

"I don't have to explain to you"

"I don't want to talk about it".

"It's not good for you".

"That's my last word on the matter".

Explain why.

"Actually I can't afford it right now, sweetie but I'll make it up to you."

Your child, no matter their age, will be able to understand your reasons, if you explain it in the language that they can grasp.

Try to provide an alternative.

If you won't permit your child to do, have or attend something, try to offer an alternative. Of course, in their eyes, that may not be as good as the real thing, but at least hopefully it may cushion the disappointment and show that you do care about their feelings. Remember even God has a prefect will and a permissive one. The perfect one is always better, though.

Remember how disappointment feels

The feeling of disappointment you feel when you don't get that job or promotion or pay rise, is the same feeling your child feels when they don't get what they want. Don't down play it and say it doesn't matter or that it's not such a big deal. It may not seem like much to you, but it definitely does to them. Try and feel what they feel. If we could measure disappointment we may find out that being dumped by a best friend can hurt as much as losing the US presidential election. Be sensitive – like Jesus was and still is. He is as understanding of our struggles, pains and weaknesses as we are.[5] He doesn't just say, "Come on girl, snap out of it". He really cares and we should too. Try to help your child get over it. When they are going about moody and sulking, sometimes you just have to let them get over their disappointment themselves. But sometimes if the melancholy is lasting a bit too long, you have to help them get over it.

The truth of life is that you win some, you lose some and you get on with life. We need to let our children know that's the way life is.

Chapter Six

The Room, the Bed and
All the Clothes on the Floor

(How do you get your children to keep their room tidy?)

The sound of the ringing bell penetrates your sub conscious and you realise that the long enjoyed sleep must come to an end. It's a quarter to six in the morning and you automatically crawl out from under the bunk bed where you sleep, to face a new day.

It's boarding school and you are a form one student at Queen's School, Ibadan, a large city in Nigeria, West Africa. It's your first year, and you are wondering why you even have to go to any school at all in the first place.

Boarding school in those days used to be like a little army camp. You were ruled by the bells. There was a bell to wake you up in the morning, a bell to start your daily morning house work – cleaning, sweeping, scrubbing floors. Then there were 3 bells to remind you that it was breakfast time, by the third one you better be on your class line in front of the dining hall. Never mind you may not want to eat that morning, you must be there or else!!! No wonder, you learnt how to be punctual for the rest of your life. They taught it to you in school.

Bells! Back to the first one. You scramble out of bed, hopefully your bucket of water that you fetched from the top up the hill is still full and you dash into the bathroom (or the area in front of the bathroom if you can't get a space inside one) to have a quick scrub. Cold water of course, unless a kind senior had helped you warm it up with an electric boiling ring.

You dress up and make your bed. That is, you make your bed, properly. Not just a quick smooth over of a bed sheet and a squeeze together of a bed cover. Your pillow is placed neatly at the top of the bed. The white bed sheet is straightened and tucked in the sides. Royal blue bed cover placed over the bed is also tucked in at the sides. Any clothes neatly put away in your locker and locked up.

You wait patiently for the dorm head to inspect before you leave for the dining hall.

You dare not leave anything out of place. You dare not.

So why do your children do just the opposite?

"Tise!!", you yell, "Do make sure you make that bed before you leave for school, (or church or football training as the case may be).

"Aw, mom, what's the point? I'm still going back to sleep on it tonight. It's going to get all roughened and rumpled up again."

"Just make it" you reply. You're not in the mood to start discussing the history of why or why beds should not be made in the morning and neither are you in the mood for an argument.

"And pick up those clothes from the floor too".

"They aren't mine mom" he starts to whine. "They belong to Tobi (or Timi or Tosho (never mind Tosho moved out 10 months ago).

They are never his. More like Mr Nobody's. Remember that poem you learnt when you were a child?

"I know a funny little man
As quiet as a mouse
Who does the mischief that is done,
In everybody's house
There's no one ever sees his face
And yet we all agree
That every plate we break was cracked
By Mr Nobody".[1]

Every house has one. Mine certainly has. It's his clothes that are littered on the floor of my son's room.

How do you get your child to keep his room tidy?

For some of them, their personality presents itself in the state of that room. If your child is well organised, a pre planner and someone who probably keeps a diary of events and things to do, her room will probably be tidy. Its just the way she is up there.

If on the other hand, your child is nearly always late, not well organised and is always getting things done at the very last minute – his room will most likely always be in a mess. It's just the way **he** is.

In boarding school they would be forced to be tidy for the consequences are dire. Kneel down, raise up your hands, fetch buckets and buckets of water from up the hill and urggh! Wash the school toilet. You didn't want to have to risk doing that. So you obey the rules. It's less painful.

But at home, it's different.

"I mean, it's only mom shouting and I can always twist her round my little finger with a smile or promise to do it when I get back from school", they say.

Depends on the mother.

For some mothers, they just simply give up. There are so many battles to fight, they give in on this one. It's not as if the children are sniffing cocaine or selling stolen goods.

Is it only a messy room? I can live with that.

But for some mothers, seeing that £100 coat peeping out from underneath the bed is a painful sight for sore eyes and they aren't having any of it.

And the way to deal with it I guess is just like you deal with so many other issues.

"If you don't tidy up that room, you're not going to school!"

(Errrm, not exactly mom, that's against the law. All children are to be in school in the UK right up until they are 16. Your child is 12.)

"If you don't tidy up that room, you're not having any dinner!!"

(Might work if you are having chicken and chips and pizza, but not if you're having broccoli and mashed potatoes.)

"If you don't tidy up that room, you're not having any Christmas presents."

(Mom, that won't work its only April and even if it was the 1st of December, that's a bit harsh and you know you won't be able to see it through")

Just bide your time. There'll probably be a school trip or a birthday party soon and they'll need your permission (and your money) to go.

So you wait patiently like a vulture, a smile curling up the sides of your mouth.

"Mom" he asks 2 weeks later, "Can I have £25 for a school trip down to the Alton Towers theme park?"

"You're not getting anything from me until................", you begin.

"Have you seen my room, mom? It's spick and span and as neat as a new pin................" he cuts in with a laugh.

Open mouth – closes.

Cheeky thing. Sometimes ....you just can't win.

Chapter Seven

Their Relationships

"You know your friend ?......"

You feel the tension already in the air.

"Which friend mum? She replies.

"You know the one. The one with the hair dyed purple"

"What about her, mum?"

You know you are treading on thin ice now and so you stall a bit, thinking maybe the time for this is not quite right.

"Nothing really..............."

There's a long pause...

You know you're still going to say something and she knows it too.

Might as well.

"Is that pure gold studded on her tongue?"

"I don't know mom", she answers.

If you're lucky she has a hint of a smile around the corner of her mouth, if you're not you can see the beginnings of a frown.

You try to say it gently.

"She seems like a very nice girl but I wonder why she dresses so outrageously".

The truth is that you can't stand the girl. Why on earth does she have such a dreadful look. Purple hair. Stud on the tongue. Urrrgh! Frightful really. You can't imagine why she is hanging around your precious daughter. You almost wish she smoked too so you could have a healthy excuse to dissuade your daughter from being her friend. You know, second hand smoke and all. But alas she doesn't.

You want to break off the friendship but you don't know how. You don't want to be considered...

Racist

Superior

Overly judgemental

Harsh

Old fashioned

Untrusting of your child's ability to have friends without being influenced by them

Truth is you are just plain nervous. Purple hair and gold stud on the tongue!! Imagine!! You dared not have a friend like that when you were growing up. Well actually, there weren't any people like that when you were growing up.

You are not going to like all their friends. Hopefully as like tends to move towards like, most of their friends will be like them. But there will be the one or the other that may be entirely the opposite. What do you do?

First of all identify why you don't like the friend. At least this one, you know about. There'll be dozens you'll never get to meet.

Is it their dressing?

Or their manners?

Perhaps they are from a different religion.

Or you just can't stand their attitude.

Their way of life seems so completely different from yours and their background is miles apart.

They are two very broad actions you could take.

First of all, you could forbid your daughter associating with her.

Depending on your child, different things may ensue.

If she's the vocal extrovert type and you have brought her up to be able to express her mind (and argue- like you do actually), she will.

"Mom, you don't even know her. Isn't that being a bit judgemental?"

Or

"Mom, is it because she's not a Christian, how am I going to win her to Christ if I don't associate with her".

Or

"Mom, how am I going to tell her that I don't want to be her friend anymore? That will be so hurtful."

And a hundred other reasons that she'll bring up.

If she's the introvert quiet type she'll just keep quiet.

Whatever type she is you cannot guarantee that she will break off the relationship.

A better action to take, should be to try and welcome their association with your child. Although it's normal to feel a bit nervous as to whether they'll influence your child's religious beliefs, you must also realise that your child may be a good influence on them and not vice versa.

The Big Book calls Christians "citizens of heaven"[1] who are just passing through this life and we are to take as many people home with us when we leave. Not via a suicide bombing. God forbid. What I mean is that while we live we should share the good news of a heavenly place being prepared for us and that we can only get in if we know and have been made right by God's Son Jesus Christ. Maybe the purple headed, tongue studded friend may be one of those you or your daughter will be bringing into that wonderful place. You never know.

Make them feel welcome when they come visiting, keep your eyes and ears open and try not to be overly critical. Be nice. You'll be surprised that she'll be turning up at your door step more often than not if you do. And that may give you a chance to find out a bit more about them and impact their lives. Better them coming over to your place than your daughter always staying out late at theirs, I'll say.

The Opposite Sex

We used to hope that our children would be all caught up with football, fashion, their faith, their school work etc that they'll be out of the university before they recognise that the opposite sex exists.

Maybe in a perfect world, that may happen. In our world? Not a chance.

My youngest son had a classmate who had a crush on him when he was 6 years old.

Though perfectly innocent, I didn't like the idea at all. She eventually faded out of the scene because her mom never used to give her a shower every day so the smell of urine put my precious son off. Thank God!

The truth is, this is a different generation than when we were growing up and the TV, internet and school associations all make it look like it's cool to have boyfriends and girlfriends as early as when you are 6 years old.

Children are being pushed to becoming adults when they are barely out of their diapers.

It's a shame really. But that's the way it is.

For instance it's Sunday School class at church and one little 6 year old chirps up, "Everybody in my class has a boyfriend except me". The poor little thing feels left out as if she doesn't belong because she didn't have a boyfriend.

"You don't need one" we reply. "You're not old enough". "Never mind, when the time is right it'll happen".

And didn't I hear just last week that a sweet little 5 year old was in love with a cute little 5 year old in her class? Excuse me?

Oh dear, you think to yourself. When we were that age we hated boys. The worst thing that could happen to you on the first day of term is to find that your teacher had put you sitting next to a boy and you are confined to that seating arrangement for the rest of the school year. What a calamity that used to be.

Not any more.

As soon as our children are able to understand we need to let them know that what is okay for adults is definitely not okay for children.

The matters of the heart are very volatile and sometimes can be deadly even for adults. Men will and have been known to kill for love and hell has no fury like a woman scorned. So as soon as our children can understand let's explain to them that no matter what the children's programmes are telling them to do, boy girl relationships are not for children.

If you pray for them earlier enough and you are lucky, they will listen to you and comply. Monitor the programmes they are watching on TV and keep your eyes and ears – physical and spiritual – open.

When they are old enough, in their late teens – probably already in university or learning some vocation or the other, it's time to have heart to heart talks with them, about long term relationships.

Our children need to be told what to look for in the man or a woman they wish to eventually spend the rest of their life with. Don't let's just assume that everything will turn out alright.

" At least," we say, "we are praying."

Good! Prayer is very important and even more so when our children are getting to that age when they will start meeting people that they'll start considering as potential future partners. Praying is very crucial but we also need to talk to them.

"Who is that young man that calls you from time to time?" you may ask.

She may say, "Aww, mom, he's just a friend. We do a couple of courses together."

Don't be fooled. Your course mate doesn't call you every day. Or are you the lecturer?

Ask relaxing not too probing questions – at least at the start.

"Really?" you reply. "...Seems like a nice guy. What is he studying?"

If she hasn't really got anything to hide, as soon as you say, "he seems like a nice guy," trust me, she'll start to talk. You just need to be sensitive enough to know what to ask and when. And when to leave off until next time!

When you don't approve ...With good reasons...

Hopefully you would have been praying for your child right from birth as regards a life partner and if you haven't you can start now.

If you have been talking regularly over the years she or he would by now know what a good future partner looks like. But alas, love is blind or so they say, and your child may fall in love with someone that you think, feel or even know is not right for them. This is a very delicate situation that must be handled with extreme care. It'll be easier to nip the relationship in the bud if you are aware before he or she falls head over heels, it'll be much harder if you aren't aware on time.

Why wouldn't you agree with your child's choice of a future partner?

We aren't talking about maybe the age gap is much wider than you and your spouse's is.

Nor are we saying one is white and the other is black. Or one's a doctor and the other's a teacher.

We are talking about him being from another faith entirely.

Or you suspecting that there is a wife or husband tucked away somewhere. (it's been known to happen)

Or maybe you have this hunch that he (or she) is just taking your child for a ride.

Whatever it is, you can't put your finger on it but you know that something is horribly and dreadfully wrong.

Marriage is for life – at least it used to be.

What do you do when you know it doesn't just feel right?

- Pray like never before. If it's not from God, He'll sort it out.
- Discuss, if possible with your child, outlining your fears and proofs if you have any.
- Get someone else to talk to her. Sometimes, someone else may be able to get through to them where you can't.
- Whatever you do, don't push them away from you. It'll be harder to get them back.

It nothing seems to be working, a time of fasting and heart rending prayer to God may be necessary. Remember He loves them, much more than you do. He formed their destiny long before they were born and will not fold His arms and let His precious child make the mistake of their lives.

He has more at stake than you ever will.

When you tell it to Him, He will sort it out.

Chapter Eight

What on Earth Do You Think You're Wearing?

*O*h my dear God, what on earth is that?

I'm at a celebration and the celebrant is all dressed up or should we say not dressed up, because actually half of her bosom is out in the open for all to see. I look around and the mini skirts that the teenagers and younger women are wearing are soooooooooooo short, it's unbelievable and frightening too. And I am not the only person making comments, the other lady at the table is too.

Later on I remark to my husband, "It's probably a good thing that we don't have any daughters", I say. "How on earth would we have been able to keep them in check".

"My daughter wouldn't dress like that", he replies. "She would have been brought up with more discipline to appreciate what is decent and what isn't"

"Hmmph. I hope so" I think to myself. "But I'm sure it's not as simple as that"

We cannot say that our children who dress inappropriately, at least by our own standards, have not been properly brought up. They don't see anything wrong in what they wear.

Mini skirts, low necked blouses showing cleavages, tight bottom hugging leggings, skin heads, mount Kilimanjaro hair cuts and sagging – all 21st century fashion.

The wisest king on earth at that time said, "See there is nothing new under the sun. All that is, has been before".[1] Well we know SYKPE and ipads are relatively new but he is kind of right as regards dressing. Minis are not new. My mother wore them in the late 50's and early 60's – not as micro as they are now though. They came back into fashion in the early 80's and are back again – it seems- to stay. Not that I have anything against the changing fashions. Life is constantly evolving. Technology, culture, demographic composition of nations, rules and regulations, in short the permissiveness of our being is sadly not static.

Only the Creator God remains the same – yesterday, today and forever.[2] Ever faithful, ever sure. It's what fashion is sometimes changing into that gives me the creeps.

There was a furor recently in the United Kingdom, about the "sexualising" of our young girls who were younger than 10 years of age by padding their bikini tops and making them look older than they really were. Some stores were selling platform shoes for children who were just eight years old.

The departmental stores in question had to apologise for the error when many parents protested.

Good for them, I say. It is about time that we do stand up for what we think is right for us and for the next generation coming after us.

The majority of people are led by certain standards and principles that govern their lives.

With a wild guess we hope that at least 99.99% believe that it's wrong to kill and that murder is the uttermost transgression someone can commit against another human being.

A lesser percentage believe that stealing is wrong also, although the definition of stealing differs from culture to culture, country to country and person to person.

For instance just because you are custodian of certain assets doesn't mean that you can put your hand in and pinch some of them, does it? Yet in some countries that is the acceptable thing to do. The perks of the job.

Anyway mode of dressing is also the same. Some people believe in modest dressing whilst some are as daring as they can be.

Even our sons seem to be on the defensive side when I make comments at a graduation ceremony or a birthday party at the plunging necklines or the micro mini skirts and dresses that seem to be the fashion these days.

"Mom," they say, "It's a different generation from yours. That's what's in the shops these days and that's why the girls are wearing them".

"But that can't be right. You don't have to buy just any trash. I hope your girlfriends won't be dressing like that."

"With a mom like ours, mom? Not a chance. They wouldn't dare".

So what do we do then, when our children seem to be dressing in a fashion that seems to be inappropriate, at least in our eyes?

I know a bit about boys and sagging – the art or science or whatever it is, of the human male species wearing a pair of trousers half way down their legs.

I hate it and resist it amongst my boys with as much effort as I can.

Not much to talk about concerning boys though is there? Their hair styles are reasonably acceptable now, though it wasn't always that way. Afros, Plateau hair cuts.

"Hmmph! Why do you cut your hair this way"? I ask.

"Mom, that's the fashion these days", they answer.

Oh well, they didn't do much after all. No earrings. No tattoos. No dreadlocks.

So I thought since I hadn't got the necessary experience to write about this issue, I'll talk to some people and make some phone calls.

I bumped into a colleague at work the other day and she asks how my book is coming.

"I'm stuck on the chapter that talks about female dressing," I reply and seize my opportunity to pick her brains about how she curtailed her daughters dressing when they were growing up.

Since my colleague Sally (not her real name) has three daughters so what better person to talk to about girls and their dressing.

"I hate those tight pants, they call leggings," she complains. "One of my daughters wears hers so tight that when she bends over to do some form of exercise, they split right down the middle."

I suppress a giggle.

"I think they're not too bad when worn under a big shirt that covers the bum area but sometimes they look like your naked body has just been painted over with black paint", I agree.

"And the shoes?" Sally continues. "They are so high, that just the other day she had to cling on to me when we are walking out in the snow. I'm a senior citizen, for heavens sake. I need someone that I can hang on to not having to prevent a vibrant young lady falling face flat in the snow."

" And pulling you down with her", I want to reply.

"And because I have three of them (and one son)", she continues, "they are always in agreement concerning their dressing. "Don't listen to mom", they say. "She's old fashioned.""

"What about the low necked cleavage revealing dresses?" I asked.

"Oh, I never really had any problems with them about that. They preferred to keep what should be hidden, hidden".

Good for you, Sally. Wish every one was like that.

What do you do and how do you imbibe Christian dressing into the heart of your budding teenage daughter?

What do you say when she tells you, "Mom, every one's wearing it. I don't want to look old fashioned and out of touch with what's the rave today".

It really starts as early as she can understand the concept of dressing neatly and decently. As early as your little girl turns 3, you should be telling her how to sit properly and how to cover up the secret parts of her body.

If a little girl is taught from an early age that her body is special, beautiful and should be treated as such, you are more likely to be successful as she grows into puberty and adult hood in getting her to see what types of dressing befit a young lady and those that don't. A Christian girl is of royal descent.[3] A daughter of the King.

Another colleague of mine, who isn't even a practising Christian was moaning to me a while ago.

"One of the reasons why I don't enjoy going into the city centre in the heat of summer, is that the women are so scantily dressed. Every thing's just hanging out", he complains.

Oh well, thank God for the winter. Everything's all covered up then.

You might score a point with your budding teenage daughter that some men don't like it either!

That may do the trick.

Chapter Nine

When One Seems
Smarter than the Other...

*G*enes and genetics – what do they mean?

In an attempt to define what a gene was I looked up Wikipedia on the internet. Wrong choice. I couldn't understand a word of the paragraphs upon paragraphs that were printed there. So I looked again and found a question put on the internet about it by a 13 year old who had a test the next day. And someone hurrah, answered and wrote, "A gene is the basic unit of heredity in a living organism."

That's good enough for me, I thought. In the simplest of terms a gene is in you that you got from an ancestor that went before you and you will most likely transfer it on to one of your descendants coming after you. So if you are Caucasian you could have red hair but neither your dad or mom or grandparents on either side may have red hair. You may have had a great aunt or uncle who was a red head and you inherited the gene in her that caused her hair to be red. So, no, your parents have not kept the secret of your adoption from you. You are their natural born daughter; it's just that you have inherited some genes that they don't have.

A genetic inheritance may be good or unfortunately bad. Some people inherit cancer from their parents; some inherit diabetes or some kind of family disease or disorder. So you hear the phrase, "it runs in the family" and in some Christian Pentecostal circles it's regarded and dealt with as a curse, breaking its hold over the carrier with positive results actually. But that's not a discussion for today.

Here we want to focus on the positive genetic inheritances like when your child is blessed enough to inherit some very good looks or better still, some very supersonic brains.

It seems so unfair when one child seems (and I emphasize on "seems") to be much more intelligent and clever than the other.

She gets the spellings all right in primary school. She is quick to learn her times tables. She eventually gets into one of the best secondary schools. Of course, she's the book worm. Always does her homework on time and a bit extra too. And makes you swell with pride at the parent/ teachers evening.

It might have been a bit better if she was the first born but not a chance- she's your second daughter.

What about your first...?

Well your first child, who is also a girl, just seems to be different from her younger sister. Doesn't really like reading that much. Just manages to scrape through her tests, kind of 51% passes most of the time. You have to check her home work most days and though she says, "We don't have any home work mom", you know they do.

What about parent / teachers evenings?

You really don't want to attend but you know you must. Its just so irritating sitting there listening to that smug teacher telling you that your precious daughter is working towards a C and even needs extra remedial classes to achieve it. She doesn't seem to like science, or geography or IT. Math? Don't even mention it. That's a disaster.

"Why can't you be more like your sister?" you complain after a trip back from one unpleasant parents/ teachers evening.

You really wish you hadn't said it but for heavens sake, you know inside of you that you wish it, so why deny the fact. At least your son, who is third born, is not too bad. Not a genius but well above average at school. Why should she be different?

Genes.......... That's why.

First of all remember that you were probably not the top of your class in your days or was it your husband that repeated class 2? Wasn't it also rumored that Uncle Sam on your father's side dropped out of university in his third year only to have to start all over again some where else?

But why your daughter has to inherit that side of the family? It's just the way it is. Just the way it's turned out and just the way the Creator made her.

"Now that doesn't sound very fair" you may think but if you stop to really think about her, you'll notice some things you never really noticed before.

She may not really like reading that much and she does need her GCSE's for sure, but doesn't she run like a gazelle and is a keep fit fanatic? While her sister is constantly munching away on whatever chocolate's available in the house, she prefers to eat apples and vegetables to keep in shape.

She hates math, yes, but she loves biology especially the parts that teach about the body make up – bones and muscle and the like. So she's probably more likely to excel as an athlete or a fitness instructor and not the doctor or lawyer you were hoping she'll be.

Don't get me wrong, if she is not pushing herself she needs to be corrected – firmly. No dilly dallying and allowing her to just laze around. She really must be stretched to achieve her highest potential. She must do the very best she can do. But we must be careful to make sure we guide her to be what she is created to be.

The Big Book cautions us about trying to be like some body else.[1] It says we are all wonderfully and beautifully crafted by the Creator in His likeness.[2] And He has made each one of us different, giving us different skills and abilities. It's silly wishing you were someone else and is a slap in the face of the One who made you the way you are.

Some of us spend a lifetime trying to discover what we can excel in. Some of us find out so very early in life. It's our duty as a good parent to help our child discover that special talent, gifting, skill that they have been endowed with and help them to develop it to its fullest capacity. Comparing one child with another just breeds dissension and bad blood amongst them. It makes the one dislike the other.

But when each child is allowed to focus and concentrate on what he or she loves doing and does almost effortlessly they are more likely to become happy well adjusted adults making a decent living from what they have been trained to do.

When a child is still a child it is important to develop the natural skills that will be necessary for living as an adult. They must know how to read and write well (some adults went through college and still can't do this properly). They must know how to do basic arithmetical sums accurately. How can she understand the financial implications of taking out a loan if she never learnt how to calculate interest on capital and the pay back amount? These lessons are very essential and your child needs to be told that she will need them later in life.

She needs to know how her body is made up, so that at puberty and woman hood she is not caught unaware when her body begins to change. There is basic knowledge that every 21st century adult is required to acquire and your child may need help to acquire them.

However as soon as you begin to notice a talent in the one, look also for another talent in the other. They are not the same. Even identical twins are different in some ways. One may be a smart scientist, the other may be a gifted artist and yet another may become a doctor. They are all smart, but in different fields. Celebrate who they have been created to be. You may not understand it. It may seem all so strange to you. It may not even be a vocation or profession that you were conversant with when you were young. Don't worry. Talk to God, educate yourself and talk to your child.

Together you can refine the gifting in them and produce a career / life that the Creator will be proud of in the end.

Don't force or push them into being what they are not.

Find out what they are.

Chapter Ten

Express Your Love

In the Big Book, there's a steamy story of love between a king and a young lady[1]. Very steamy actually. If you are religious you may wonder what that kind of story is doing in such a revered Book.

I think the story is there not only to actualise the love the Creator has for His creation, but to cover love between the different classes of His people. Husband and Wife, Brother and sister, mother in law and daughter in law, Mother and Daughter, Father and Son etc. Even friends.

The Creator, God – is love. He loves us so much that He will freely give us any thing we need and He expects us to love the same way, if possible. Unconditionally[2].

You may say, "That's nothing new. I love my child – very much. I support her, buy her clothes, pay for trips abroad, even pray for her regularly".

Good. Very good. Love is expressive. When we love we show that we love. By what we do for one another. Or what we say to one another. Or how we touch each other.

How do you express love to your child?

Touching.

A hug?

A Kiss?'

A Cuddle?

Holding a hand?

It's sad that we lose the ability to touch our children when they grow up even though we spent the first 3 to 4 years of their lives holding them close to ourselves. The minute they are out of the womb we are carrying, holding them close to our bodies, breast feeding them, comforting them when they cry, rocking them to sleep, carrying them in a monkey carrier or if you are African or Asian, tying them snugly to our backs.

It seems however that as soon as they learn to walk confidently on their own or the next baby comes along, we become a little bit more and more distant as the years roll by. Soon we hardly have that much body contact at all.

Body contact is good for your child. A simple gesture like placing your hand lightly on his head, whilst leaning over to pour milk into a cereal bowl says, "I recognise that you are sitting down here and want to acknowledge your presence."

Or

"I'm a little tired, you provide a little stability for me when I lean over. Thanks for being there".

If you are not used to expressing love this way, it doesn't mean you don't love your child, it's just a good way of showing it and it's never too late to start. Even if they are already grown up.

Hugging a child could interprete to mean "My body is precious to me, one of the most precious things I own. When I hug you I'm sharing myself with you".

One of my sons introduced his lady friend to me once and I was in a church gathering where a lot of people knew me and wanted to say hello. Even though I had spoken to her a number of times on the phone, this was my first time of meeting her in person and I knew she would be nervous. Amidst the hustle and bustle of other people wanting to say hello, I reached out and held on to her hand whilst I said hello to a couple of other people. My touch reassured her that "even though I am not saying hello to you right now, I know you are waiting to speak to me and I am holding your hand to acknowledge that." I got brownie points from my son, for that!!

Could it be that when we are not physically connected to our children, they look for it outside, elsewhere in the wrong place?

Praise and celebrate your child

When you praise and celebrate your daughter for every little achievement, in the future when men start chatting her up, trying to get a leg in the door, she will be able to say, " that's not a big deal, my dad has said that to me a hundred times". She does not need to crave for endearments, she's already used to being praised and commended. It's not likely she'll fall for every hook, line and sinker that men drop by her way.

"Oh sweetie, you are so fine. Has any body told you how beautiful you are?" they say.

"Actually, yes", she replies . "A thousand times".

What she's saying is that, I know that already. My dad and mom have been saying it to me since I was two. So try another line, fella.

When any of my boys complain that they are too black, I tell them, "you are so handsome, just the way you are. God has made you perfectly. You don't need to change a thing".

Praising your child gives them the confidence they need to make a bold start in life. They will go through many firsts. First day at school. First day at the University. First day at work. First day they'll set their eyes on their future spouse. Your years of commendation will help them feel good about themselves. That doesn't mean that you overdo it and make them feel good even when they are not performing up to standard. They will face and have to meet targets in life and when they don't, they will learn that there are consequences. But when they do well, tell them.

Listen and learn

As soon as your child is born the teaching process begins. You are not only teaching him, he's teaching you too.

You never learnt baby language in its depth before you became a parent. You never knew how to work out when a baby is tired, wet or hungry before, did you? Your baby taught you.

You know, I wonder what goes on in a baby's mind when they are crying.

"Mom, please don't be daft" they scream, "I can't be hungry yet. I had a bottle of milk just half an hour ago. I'm definitely soaking wet, mom. If you remember I told you the same thing yesterday. You only have to reason it out properly and I wouldn't have to keep screaming my head off".

Or she may be thinking, "Dancing with me across the sitting room is not going to make me feel better, lady, all I want is some peace and quiet. Peace and quiet!! Not Tom Jones' Delilah.

Or your baby son may be trying to tell you that, "Mom, the nappy is too tight. I'm a boy, not a girl!!"

And you have to figure it out for yourself.

And so day after day, we teach and they learn, they teach and we learn. It's really no different as they get older.

One thing I have definitely learnt from my sons is that I can never keep up with the changing scenes of technology. I'm always asking "how do you do this or how do you do that?" And some things I don't even bother to learn, I just wait for them to come home and do it for me. I still have the old phone I've had for about 7 years now, I think, because I can't be bothered to try out a better one. We don't have to wait until they are in their late teens or early twenties before we appreciate that we can learn a lot from them. Let's face it, we don't know it all. And even though we told them that we were always first in the class examinations when we were young, they'll soon find out as they grow older, that we weren't. We know a lot, agreed, by virtue of the number of years we have lived on the earth, but there are so many new nouvelle things we don't have a clue about.

Allow your child the excitement of teaching you something, once in a while. Laugh with them at your mistakes and sometimes don't let on that you know more than they think you do. Listen to their opinion even when they are only ten and more especially when they are thirteen and struggling through that stage of puberty when they moan "you never listen to what I have to say".

Of course, you are the boss, no doubt about that, and they must learn that as early in life as possible. But it won't hurt to let them lead, once in a while.

Another thing I've learnt across the years is that when you love your children, they will love you back. And when they have flown the nest they will want to come back. When they call you on their mobile phones from University, using up their precious phone credits just to say things like...

"How are you mom?".

"I just wanted to find out how you are doing".

"Hope you are having a good day, dad".

"I so miss you guys".

"You know what mom, I do love you".

Doesn't it all seem so worthwhile?

Chapter Eleven

Making Sweet Memories

"Time and tide wait for no man", the saying goes.

The days fly past very quickly and before we know it we pass from young mother to middle aged mother to grandmother and hopefully great grand mother (or father as the case may be).

There was a time when the store keeper would address you as "young lady", when you paid for your groceries at the check out.

Now it's definitely "Thank you, madam. Hope you have nice day"

Wonder where the "young lady" went?

Can't fool any one – even with the hair dyed black and all.

Time is flying and that is why we have to cherish the moments, the days as they come. We'll never get them back.

That's why when I meet a colleague at the kitchen sink at work and they say" thank God it's Friday", I always try to reply "yes, thank God, but remember you're also a week older. Don't wish your life away".

If we realise that we can't get back those years to live them again, why not let's try and make some memories as we go along.

It's never too late to start. Even if your children are already in boarding school or University or even if they are already married it's never too late to start making memories. At one stage of our lives that may be the closest thing we have left.

Do things together with your children. Things they like to do if possible. Doesn't have to be so expensive. Go watch a movie or eat out at a fish and chips shop or once in a blue moon take a holiday together. Make memories. Take photographs and preserve them as much as possible. Later on in life they'll bring so much joy to your heart.

Do things together. It's not always about making money. It's more important to build relationships and bind ourselves to one another.

This summer our family all travelled back to Nigeria after, for 5 of us, 11 years of sojourning in England. It was my dad's 80th birthday. So the entire clan met up for Grandpa Adetona Balogun's 80th birthday and our first son's traditional wedding which we call an engagement or betrothed ceremony.

It was like heaven. We had the best time ever. All five children and spouses and grand children gathered together at our

"Southfork"[1] for 2 weeks for the reunion of a life time. It was so great. The memories? They will remain with us for a lifetime.

There are some things that money cannot buy. You have to create them yourself. Memories are made of these times. When each generation gets older and passes on to the next life, those left behind can still sit in front of the fire or in the open warm evening air and reminisce about the wonderful times we shared together with those whom we loved.

The trip to Nigeria cost us quite a lot of money but it was worth it. However you don't necessarily have to splash out each time you want to spend some memorable moments with your children. You'll be surprised how little it can cost to drive North, South, East or West of where you live, rent a cheap hotel if need be and find some things to do in the town or the city you choose to drive to.

Take some photographs or make some videos and just have some fun. Try and forget about the bills, the job and even the ministry if you head one and enjoy each other's company.

Mobile phones off. Laptops off. Lock yourself out of the world and into your family.

Make some memories.

When you remember them tomorrow, you can bring yesterday back to today.

Chapter Twelve

Let the Children Come to Me and ... Talk!

his book is for parents primarily, parents to be and maybe teenagers might enjoy a chapter or two. However my husband, Pastor Niyi, suggested, "Why don't you set a side a chapter for young people and the still young at heart to be able to give their opinions and experiences and challenges. How their growing up years have been".

I thought that seemed like a good idea and so this chapter is for them to say a few things about their growing up years and their parents.

Some names have been changed but some have allowed me to quote them verbatim.

As we all know we are all different. God fashioned us differently so that there'll be a lot of variety. Some teenagers are very bubbling and exuberant. Whilst some are very quiet and reserved, as I found out. Their personality kind of determined how their teenage years panned out.

Teenage Self Consciousness

What for instance makes a young girl shy. Could be just a natural in built personality or it could be an external experience.

Jayne for instance remembers how self conscious she was about her appearance during her teenage years. She was a naturally shy person, so going through adolescence made things a little bit tricky. Never one of those outspoken, popular kids at school, she just preferred to melt into the background.

"And then I remember the day I cracked my front tooth during a swimming session and 3/4 of it fell out."

(Isn't that a coincidence, I did that too running up the school stairs to put my school bag down for a quick tumble on the climbing frame, just before school started. And oww! Didn't that hurt!)

Mortified, Jayne remembers she couldn't even talk for a whole week at school for fear of revealing a wide gapping toothless smile.

We've all attended primary and secondary school so you know the phrase "Gappy tooth" would probably follow you for the rest of your life!

So a very shy person just had to become even shyer until the tooth got properly and permanently fixed many years later.

As parents, do we ever wonder if we have gotten it wrong or right?

Do we know or care about what our children think about our ways and methods of bringing them up?

Are we brave enough to ask what they think or couldn't we care less?

Let's listen to a few of them.

Better than I could have chosen myself...

Maxine Johnson is a final student at Keele University, Staffordshire, England.

" I love my parents!!" she says.

" I wasn't raised up in Christ as my parents were not what we would title as 'saved'; in spite of this they gave me the best childhood and kept me in check during my teenage years. My father is not my biological dad, and yet no one would ever know any different as he treats me as equal as his own blood. My parents and I have a close relationship and I believe I can approach them about anything, even if on the surface it may appear to be a bit of an 'awkward' conversation. I call home every evening to reassure them that all is well at Uni, and I see them every weekend; maybe a bit too much for a student. . . "

"No, I'm just kidding!! I appreciate what they have taught me in life, both expressly and impliedly. I am thankful to God and so much blessed to be gifted with such amazing parents. I think they are doing a great job and cannot suggest any major reforms for them to improve."

Halleluya! Isn't that just so sweet! A loving mom and a step dad, that's even better than a dad. Hurrah!

What about Communication?

Seyi was blessed enough to be born just few years after his parents converted from Muslims to Christians, and they later went on to become pastors. He was therefore brought in a Christian home. The second born of two sons, his parents had a close relationship with him.

"My parents have always treated both of us the same even though I wonder sometimes who is their favourite. Sometimes you feel like asking but I guess it's best not to know".

"As we have grown older, over the last few years I feel like both my brother and I, have grown closer to my mum than was the case when we were younger. She is starting to recognise that we are now young adults rather than the kids we used to be. I like it because it's easier now to talk freely with her either when we are at home or at school".

""They are always calling you on the phone" my dad complains to my mum. "They never ring me"".

"I really love my dad. He's always been there for me but sometimes I feel he still regards us as kids and relates to us as such.

That's probably why we lean more to mom who treats us more like adults. Could be because he's very reserved with people and so doesn't talk that very freely.

Whenever we are together especially when, I get the chance to travel down to Nigeria, we have very nice times together. I really cherish those times. And I look eagerly forward to when I can speak to him for hours on the phone instead of just about twenty seconds as we do now. Hopefully that will come with time.

What can I say about my parents? Seyi asks. Wonderfully God fearing, I have learnt so much from them. When I hear people complain that their parents were never there for them, I thank God for mine. They have always been and hopefully will always be there for me for as long as possible.

And if they ever get to read this book, I want them to hear me say "dad, mom. . . . .thank you!!""

First Child... First to say Thanks

"In my household I would forever remain 16 in the eyes of my parents!" Renee remembers.

"I was always seeking my space, my freedom and as the first child I thought I deserved every right to it".

"I remember the times I'd swear not to bring my kids up with the "supposed" same strong hand with which I was brought up.

I'm going to let them stay out late.

I'm never going to be as restricting as my folks were."

Those were my thoughts while I was growing up but now with a more informed perspective reflecting on things and yes with a bit of maturity, I now realise how very much similar to them I will be. May be even worse (or should I say "better"!).

(Renee's kids - watch out!)

At times you'd wish your parents were less into your business and would just 'bug off' but trust me as you and they get older you realise how much you want them around, realising that all along they had always had your best interests at heart. (How sweet!)

Being young parents and raising 5 "munchkins", must have been really tough on them and it's now that I can imagine what it must have been like. But God was definitely on their side and with Him, everything was and is still very possible.

I can proudly say I am VERY fortunate to be blessed with my wonderful and supporting parents of whom without, I definitely wouldn't be where I'm now! I know I can never say it enough but I am saying it now. Dad and mom, I sincerely LOVE and appreciate you and for the record, I'd take being treated as a 16 year old over the responsibilities that come with being 21 in my household anytime!

Daddy's tomboy...Mom's Woman

Lola's parents live just over 4000 miles away.

"I don't get to see them as often as I'd like", she reminisces, "but when we do get together, we have an amazing time and I cherish every moment".

I suppose the distance between us makes me appreciate the sacrifices they make for me and my sisters, daily, and it motivates me to be the very best I can be; I want them to be proud of me - in everything I do.

My relationship with my parents is kind of paradoxical. I'm closer to my dad, probably because I'm a 'tomboy' and he's the "hip" parent. The older I get however, the closer my mum and I become. Could be because I'm blossoming into a young woman or maybe it's because I finally realise all her "Lola act like a lady" talks, come from a place of love. . . Who knows?

I appreciate my parents. For who they are as individuals, for their personalities - and for the role they decided to take on - raising me and my sisters. Mom, dad, this is your Lola saying, "I love you!".

And it's never too late to get closer

Oredola is the last of 3 kids and was raised by both her parents.

"My mother was my best friend when I was a kid," she remembers, "and I did not like being away from her but she got posted to another part of the country for work, and so we kind of grew apart."

"Because dad was nearby I think I became closer and confided more in him".

"Then boarding school came along and I only got to see my mom once in about 2 months so things didn't really change."

"I'm grown up now though and things are thankfully getting better and I have decided to make more of a conscious effort. Brought up in a good, God fearing home, the discipline they gave me when I was much younger, has made me, I hope, develop into a strong, mature and somewhat independent lady. Life is a lot about choices, the decisions we make, and the repercussions and results of which we would have to live with.

I have since realized that mom has always in fact been there for me from afar, even though as a kid I never saw it. I see it now and I'm making a conscious effort to form a closer relationship with her even though we are even physically more further apart than we were."

"So mom, this is for you. You are the epitome of a woman and I would love to be like you when I grow up. To tell my children all sorts of fun stories about you and hear them say "oh mummy, you and grandma are soooo alike.. it's weird".

"Obviously," I'll reply. "What else should you expect? Grandma is my mother after all.."

I could never understand the rules...

Did you ever think whilst you were growing up, "I can't wait to leave this house, have my own flat and do what I like.

It'll be great to have my own job and spend my money on whatever I want. Just like Simba in Lion King – I just can't wait to be king.

Whilst she was growing up, Paris sometimes thought to herself, "One day I will have a say in this house or even stay away long enough to be terribly missed, just to be able to prove a point.

"With my parents," she says, "I never really understood the unwritten rules that had been set."

"I thought they never let me have any fun, always trying to thwart my well earned right to have a fun filled rollicking childhood".

Being the last of four children, a brother and three sisters, you can imagine four different flavoured and coated personalities running through our home. My parents operated a hierarchical system and like many other households the last born remains the last born ... forever.

Actually even now, my dad repeatedly reminds me that until I am married with at least three children of my own, I will forever be 'the baby of the house'.

My mum thinks a little bit differently. In her case she has no conditions. Married with kids or not ...I am always going to be her baby and that's that!

I'm my mum's biggest fan and we are more like '6&7', 'two peas in a pod'. I'm definitely a 'mummy's girl'. And though I know she'll never admit it, I like to hope that I'm her favourite child. She is loving, caring, full of life, and has the tremendous ability to play mum and dad (sometimes) so very well. I hope to one day become a woman like her.

And my dad? I love him too. As I get older the bond and respect for him gets stronger. I love and cherish them so dearly! More than they may realize. Sacrifices they have made so freely - emotional, physical, time and financial investments alone all make me want to be a better person for myself and for my future kids to look up to me the way I do to them.

And one of the ultimate goals is to show them the gratitude in my heart for all they have done, and how wonderfully they have raised me.

Mom, dad, you are the best. I will not trade you for anything in whole wide world!!!

Sometimes understanding comes later.....

As Jesunifemi admits sometimes children do not see things the way their parents do.

Understandable. . . because they are children.

"I'm thankful for the parents I have" she says.

"I didn't get to understand them fully until very recently. I've always known that they wanted the best for us children, but I couldn't see things from their perspective for a long time.

Each time I got reprimanded for doing wrong they would say, 'We love you and want the best for you'.

Hard to believe and so I just never seemed to agree with any of their rules and always seemed to get into more trouble.

There were times I wished I wasn't born into my family because I felt like there were unreasonable with their rules. But times passes and I have realised why they discipline us the way they do. I'm older, wiser and more appreciative of them much and life in general.

Now I honestly believe their parenting skills have shaped me into the person I am today.

A lot has been said Mom and Dad.

So if you ever wondered if it was worth all the hassle...now you know!

Chapter Thirteen

Sow a Good Seed,
Reap a Good Harvest

Create a good atmosphere for your child

Life is full of challenges. The Big Book says a righteous man – yes even a righteous man – falls seven times but gets up again.[1] So even when we are living the best way we can, things happen to us that we did not anticipate or bargain for. It's the result of living in a fallen world.

Marriages go sour and break ups happen. People get divorced. Spouses die.

Things change us. Good experiences make us feel better and help us to become better people.

Bad experiences can make us bitter and disillusioned. It's just a natural reaction to a broken world. But no matter what has happened in the course of our lives, we have to be very careful not to let our bad experiences rub off on our children. They learn very fast and pick up vibes very easily and as much as it lies within us, we have to create an atmosphere that is conducive and loving for them

Had a bad day at work?

Wish your boss would get another job and never walk through those double doors again?

Didn't get that promotion?

Drop it at the office door. Don't bring it home. Don't take it out on your children.

Is your marriage going through a bad patch? Keep the arguments as low key as possible or go for a drive, park the car and yell at each other as much as you want. Well actually I'm not sure if that's a good idea, you might get so worked up you may crash the car on the way back.

Bringing up children in a contentious atmosphere just scars them – sometimes for life.

Some children turn out to be aggressive and difficult to live with. Some don't know how to communicate properly and think until you start shouting at your companion you can't get your views across.

Some are afraid that any relationship they may go into will end up like yours and so they shun marriage completely.

Others may just learn how to be secretive in the home and to connive, lie or cheat because they see you do it to your spouse.

"Mom, Dad said this and that but don't let him know I told you or else he'll start yelling and I'll get the blame for it".

Don't put your child in between you during your marital squabbles.

This book isn't about marriage but the Big Book describes a wise man or woman as one who is able to keep their anger in check.[2] Or someone who, though quite strong is also very meek. Meek means gentle. A gentle giant. Someone who doesn't throw his/her weight around and create an atmosphere of strife and fear in the home.

You want to create a peaceful atmosphere in the home?

Try not to let your child have to choose between the two of you.

Think about them for a change. What's best for them. We took that oath unconsciously as soon as seed was passed and they were conceived. Now it's not about us. It's about them, the next generation. It's about our descendants. It's about making sure they are fully equipped to carry the baton and hand it over to the generation coming after them.

Some children really have had it bad. I was talking to a colleague the other day and she was telling me the realities of the world out there. Young children forced out of their homes at an early age, struggling to keep alive on the streets. Stealing, doing drugs, prostituting their bodies, all in an attempt to stay alive. Children whose parents do not understand that the minute you bring a child into the world you are responsible to the child for everything that it is in your power to do for him.

If you are a single parent looking to get married, your child comes first. If your proposed partner cannot love you with your child he or she is not worthy of you. No matter how lonely or vulnerable you may be, your decision must include first and foremost the welfare of your child. Too many children have been raped, abused or even killed by a partner who could not love the mother and the child she had in tow.

If you are blessed to have a child, know that they are many who would love to have that privilege, please, take care of that child. One day whether we believe it or not, God, the God of that child will call you to account concerning what you did to help that child through life.

It's a jungle out there, we all know it and though we hope and pray that our children will slide through it smoothly, we would be fooling ourselves if we never thought that they would face some form of challenge as they do. It's just the world we live in.

The best we can do is to try and make their formative years as stress free and peaceful as possible. Do the very best you can do and God will do the rest.

A few months ago just as this book was being written we were trying to understand and comes to terms with the sad and devastating massacre of 20 children and 6 adults in Connecticut in the United States of America. The gist of the story is that a 20 year old man shot and killed his mom in her pyjamas and then took her guns and headed for a primary school in the area. By the time he shot himself dead, he had murdered 26 people. Of that number 20 of them were children between the ages of 6 to 7 years of age. All cut down before their lives could really begin.

How do you anticipate this kind of tragedy?

How can you prevent it happening again?

How can you ensure you child does not grow up to become the perpetuator of such a dastardly crime?

Can you know what is going on in the mind of your children?

May be not but by speaking to your child, showing them love, you can find out what life is planting in their minds. Hopefully we can influence what germinates and grows in there.

Hopefully we can nip any evil seed before it is full blown and fully rooted in the soil of their minds. Before it can be a threat to themselves, you and the community at large.

Parents, we need to sow good seeds. There is so much to be done in our generation, in our world, to safe guard the lives of our children. There is so much to be done to steer them carefully and safely through life.

Massive sacrifices must be made, undoubtedly.

Make them.

Your children will never forget what you did give up for them. And one day you will reap a seven fold harvest.

Shalom!

Chapter Fourteen

Your Faith

*B*eing a Christian, you would expect that some where in this book I would kind of, mention it and now I am.

If you aren't a Christian, Ill like to explain, in nutshell who a Christian is or is supposed to be.

A Christian believes in God and that this Father God, who we have been calling Creator, God Father on and off in this book, sent His Son Jesus the Christ to the world to save the world from their sins and reconcile us back to Himself.[1]

Christians believe that Jesus died on the cross, was crucified actually, rose up from the dead on the third day and eventually went back to heaven. We believe that His coming and leaving has given us a new lease of life and that we can live a godly prosperous life here on earth and eventually get to meet and live with God in heaven.

In a nutshell that is the Christian faith. We believe it, live it and teach our children to live it also.

If you are a Christian (and I am hoping that if you're not yet one, you will become one very soon), you should bring up your child (children) in the way of the Christian God. To the best of your ability, you must endeavour to make sure that when they reach the age of accountability, they will decide to live their lives for Christ. It is our duty as Christian parents and the Almighty God expects us to pursue this mandate to the best of our ability. The children that have been given to us by God are not really ours. We can say we are guardians or as we say here in England foster parents or custodians. God says "Here, I give you my child to look after, to nurture and to love. I expect you to help him reach his fullest potential in life. I expect you to teach him about me. And I will require from you an account at the end of time".

Hmmmph!

A very sacred and awesome commission to ask of you, but He asks of it anyway and He will hold us accountable for how that child turns out when we pass from this world into the next.

So how can we make sure we do our very best to ensure we give the children back to God in a state that He will be pleased with our efforts?

Start when they are young. You can't do it on your own

Help them to get to know the living God themselves

Make Christianity exciting for them. With changing technology almost everything is changing with it. God never changes but the way we present Him to our children may have to. Invest in Christian teaching aids that make the stories in the Big Book come alive and captivating.

Bring them up within a church family. Help them grow up with other children just like themselves. Let them form relationships within the church as they will form relationships in school and other secular environments. If there aren't children or young people of their own age groups in your church, they are not likely to want to go there. And if the church has no department for teenagers they are going to find it extremely boring even if you seem to like it.

Explain why they cannot do what every body else is doing. Tell them that they are sons and daughters of the King and she carry themselves appropriately.

Give them examples from the world around them.

When they are old enough, let them know the blessings and rewards of Christianity and all they have to lose also, if they reject it.

Be a good shining example to them. Do what you are teaching them to do. Don't live a life of a double standard. Let them follow you as you follow Christ.

More important of all, pray for your children as often as you can. Pray that they will have a good life, that they'll grow up to be God fearing well adjusted young men and women, that you and the world can be proud of.

Chapter Fifteen

Your Time

No matter how much you love your child you must find some time to be away from him and chill out. You need your own time once in a while, even if it's just for a night and a day, to refresh yourself and relax. Remember before you were a parent you were a person. And when your child leaves home you'll still be that person. Find the time and the expense that goes with it to get away even if it's just once a year and be by yourself or with adult friends.

If you are married you can go away with your spouse, If not spend sometime with your friends. Possibly friends like you who also have children.

The word is "escape" from them all and live your life for a day or so.

So if it's that annual women's Christian conference that says you can bring the children along – refuse to do that. DON'T take them. Arrange for a reliable help to stay with them for a day or two, if you can afford to and fly away into a day or two of freedom.

When our boys were old enough we used to leave them at home during the annual ministers conference from Thursday afternoon to Saturday afternoon. We were away from them, but actually we weren't really. With that wonderful contraption called a mobile phone, we, actually I, was on the phone checking them out every now and then. And I was not alone. I'd sneak out to find a quiet place to make a call and find two, three, ten other mothers doing just the same thing. Calling home.

Later that night at about eleven o'clock you're calling home again.

"Are you home?"

"No mom, we're out clubbing", a sleepy voice replies.

Silly question when you've just called the house phone.

"I meant are you in bed?"

"Yes mom".

"Did you put off the light?"

"Yes Mom".

"The TV?"

"Yes Mom".

"The iron?"

"Yes Mom".

"Did you lock the door?"

"Mom! Go to sleep. We are fine"!

You try to get to sleep, listening to your husband's deep, sleep breathing (snoring actually) and wonder how on earth he can sleep so peacefully, whilst you are worried, almost to death about the children left at home.

The second day away is a school day – Friday – so you wake up at 2am, 3am, 4am, 5am and at 6.30 am you are out of bed and ringing home. Brring brrrrng!

"Wake up!" you say as soon as someone picks up the phone. "You'll be late for school".

"No we won't mom, we've already had a shower and are getting dressed".

"Oh".

Surprised that they can do that on their own?

"Errm, have you had a shower?"

"Yes, mom, I just told you that".

"What about breakfast?".

"We will mom, when we finish getting dressed".

"Is it raining? Make sure you keep warm today the weather forecast is that it'll be very cold".

"Mom, you just leave us alone and enjoy your conference. We will be just fine. Okay".

"Okay" you reply, a little bit despondent and wondering how on earth they can manage without you.

Well actually, they can.

Is it wrong to do what you do?

No, it isn't. That's why you are a parent. But you really do need to take time off to be on your own. Do things for yourself. Learn to enjoy your own company. One day when they all leave home, you will have to. Just like you did before they came along into your life.

Do you ever wonder what you were doing with your self before you became a parent?

Try and remember what it was and do it again. Live a few days of the year for yourself.

Chapter Sixteen

Do You Have to Talk About Sex?

*G*ood question. Do you have to talk to your teenagers about sex? Many parents may not want to. You think to yourself, "My parents didn't tell me anything when I was their age".

Probably not, because you were born in the sixties and parents didn't talk about that kind of thing – openly - then.

The best kind of counsel a young African girl could get about sex, back then was when she started having her monthly periods.

Let's imagine the situation. She's trying to come to terms with the not so pleasant fact that she'll be going through this uncomfortable and most times, painful process each month for the next forty to fifty years or more, and what does her mother say?

"Now you are a young woman, I mustn't see you next to any boy! Do you understand me! If you move near any boy, you'll get pregnant and your life will be ruined! And don't think I'm here to look after any baby at my age. I've done my own bit. I'm warning you now. Let it not be said that I didn't warn you! Blah! Blah! Blah!"

Confused young and thirteen is even more confused after that tirade. What on earth was that all about? Is what is happening to me, a bad thing? Does she mean no more talking to boys? No more studying together with boys? No more playing basket ball with boys? What about sitting next to boys in class? Definitely not! Might get pregnant. And when it's the end of year school party, no dancing! That may be very dangerous. So we see Young and Confused unfortunately, has to find out the real truth about sex and relationships from friends who really don't know the correct way to explain it to her.

That was then you say.

Okay maybe that was the case in the sixties and seventies. Things have changed considerably these days, though. Today what happened to you when you start your monthly menstruation periods and sex education is taught in schools – to some children as early as eleven years old.

"So", you may say, "they'll learn about it in school. I don't really have to teach them anything".

Hmmm! Yes and no. If your child is taught sex education in school, at an age you believe is far too early, it may be safe to sit them down and find out what exactly has been told to them and straighten out any grey or uncertain areas. If your child seems nervous or shy to discuss it with you, it means he or she is not ready and you may have to bide your time and wait a little.

Boys may be more likely to want to discuss such sensitive issues with their dad. Girls with their mom. But there's no hard and fast rule about who does it. And there's no point pushing the responsibility to each other.

"You're her mother, you talk to her."

"Why should it be me? You're her dad and she's closer to you. You talk to her".

"I don't know what to say."

"Neither do I".

Keeping quiet about the whole thing hoping she'll hang on to the "Birds and the Bees" story until she's twenty? You know that isn't going to help.

You've got to talk to her sometime. Sooner than later. Before an amorous young man gets into her mind ... and her heart first.

Or if it's a him. Before he is sexually trapped in the arms of a woman more than twenty years older than himself.

One of the reasons that we do have to speak to our children as soon as possible is because your child needs to be protected. Any innocent child can be a prey to a paedophile, a rapist or any type of child molester. Our children need to be aware, as I have earlier reiterated, of the dangers out there. Sadly for some young people and children, the danger is closer than we think.

There's the story in the big Book that could as well have been pulled out of a 21st century soap opera.

The nation of Israel, at that time had a great king. His name was David. Remember David and Goliath? That's him.

Well, David if you remember had quite a number of wives, sons and daughters. Or princes and princesses as we should call them. Some were just averagely good children and you don't read a lot about them but a few of them were a nasty piece of work.

One of these very nasty pieces of work was a young man who had a crush of one of his half sisters, his sister from another mother. In ancient Israel at that time you were allowed to marry your sister, if she was not born by your mother. So he develops a crush on this pretty young Tamar and acting on the advice of his brother lures her into his tent on the pretext of being unwell... and rapes her.

When he has satisfied his evil carnal desire, the love (or should we say lust?) he had for her turns to hate and he drives her out from his presence.

He eventually gets what's coming to him but alas, he's destroyed the young woman's life, because after that terrible incident, who's going to want her now? There's not much of a second chance for a disvirgined princess in ancient Israel[1.]

Our children need to be told that there is sexual danger out there and that they should be very careful to avoid it.

Another reason why we should speak to our children as soon as possible is because children themselves can be very precocious. And experimental too. Once a boy realises that his body is different from a little girls he wants to look and find out why. They need to be told that it is a sin and a crime against the law to touch someone else. Some of these young ten to twelve year olds just don't know what is wrong and what is right. We need to tell them before they are handed down a sentence in a law court.

There's of course the issue of sexually transmitted disease that young people and even adults are often ignorant of.

ID is a dentist in St Albans, just outside London. Because she has always had a great relationship communication wise with her children, the sex talk just flowed through naturally. Of course there were the earlier puberty talks on cleanliness and coming of age in both her daughter and her son, when they were younger.

Looking back she recalls a TV programme they were all watching about Sexually Transmitted Diseases when the children were about sixteen and fourteen years old respectively. She seized the opportunity to hit the nail on the head and talked to them about sex.

Outlining the Biblical reasons from abstaining from pre marital sex she explained the physical and medical reasons also. Curable. Incurable. Infertility. Death sentence. Because of their close knit relationship, any feeling of embarrassment was non existent.

Every child is different and comes to maturity at different times. So also the time for the "sex talk" will also differ from child to child. Some children will make it easy for you and ask you out right what they want to know. Some may be too shy to ask but you do perceive that they have questions that need to be answered sooner than later.

I don't think there is any easy way to broach the subject. You'll just have to ask the Holy Spirit for help. ...And tread softly.

Karen (not her real name) has been speaking to her children about sex since they were about ten. In a rather blatant way she would say, " It's what your daddy and I do together, or I'm the only one allowed to have sex with your father". Ouch! I thought that was a bit too direct for a child of ten. But it did seem to have worked for them.

I recall an article I read once where daddy told his sixteen year old daughter, "Mom and I will be using the den tonight and do not want to be disturbed."

With a knowing look in her eye, she asks "And what will I see if I come into the den tonight, dad?"

"You'll find your mom and I lying naked together in front of the fire, that's what"!

Now that's direct! I'd faint if my husband said that. But this sixteen year old was definitely not confused, and must have had some awareness of the matter. I guess little quirks like that do pave the way for the great talk.

I 'm coming in from a women's prayer and social evening and find that my husband has bought some chicken, skinned and chopped and has even parboiled it in readiness for me to cook! Halleluya!

I walk into the living room and give him a big kiss.

"Hey," I announce to Tobi (second born) and Tise (the baby), "Daddy deserves a big kiss for all that work and even something else later!"

"Awww mom", Tobi moans, "That's kind of embarrassing. You're making me close my eyes".

Tise doesn't say a word.

It's later on as he wanders into my room that he asks,

"Mom?"

"Yes sweetie", I answer absent minded.

"Mom, how many times in a week do you and daddy......you know?"

Oh my God, I panic, what on earth is he asking?

And what should I say? Should he be allowed to ask me that?

Caught unawares I reply, "Well actually you really shouldn't be asking me that question. It's kind of intrusive."

And then thinking I've not given the right answer I ramble on with a load of silly answers.

"Ask your dad". And then I say...

"No, he'll be offended". And then I say...

"You don't need to know about that now". And still then I say...

"When the time is ripe I'll talk to you about it".

The boy is going on for nineteen, for heaven's sake. When will the time be ripe?

Maybe if we'd had the talk together years ago, hubby and I wouldn't have spent the last ten years or so creeping around on lover's night, listening to see if the children were safely down stairs watching TV or sound asleep in bed.

A simple talk would have definitely have kept them out of sight, instead of the once a while knocking on our locked door and asking, "Why did you lock the door?"

Don't leave it too late like I seem to have.

"Tosh", I ask my twenty six going on twenty seven soon- to-be-married first born son, "Don't you think we need to talk to you about sex"?

He laughs.

"Mom, it's a bit late for that now, don't you think? I'll be married in 2 months".

Yeah, I guess so.

Better start early with the others then.

Early? The others are almost twenty three, twenty one and nineteen.

Thank God their dad has spoken to them. Strange though, since I talk to them about everything else. I wonder how I left this very important thing out.

Probably unconsciously didn't want to.

One of you has to.

Soon.

Who will it be?

Chapter Seventeen

Flying the Nest

Preparing Yourself
Boarding School

It's sometime in September 1997 and our first son, now eleven years old, is off to boarding school – far away (in my opinion) on the borders of the town in which we live.

It seemed like a good school when we chose it and we were happy when he was accepted but as soon as we dropped him off, I began to feel the ache in my heart.

"Why did you chose that school?" I began to nag my husband. "it's too far away. It's near the Republic du Benin".[1]

The Republic du Benin is the next country to the west of Nigeria where we lived then.

"What if there's war between us and them? What if they come and massacre our children? What if? What if? What if?"

"He'll be okay," he replies.

"Yeah, he'll be okay. It's okay for you to say that. You didn't carry him for nine months in your belly. You didn't push and push in so much pain till he came shooting out. You didn't breast feed him, wipe his nose and carry him on your back. Nag. Nag. Nag" I reply silently in my mind.

"Trust me. He'll be okay," he reassures me again.

You need to know something about my husband, Niyi.

A pastor of one of our RCCG churches in England, nothing ever bothers him. The house could be on fire and the roof falling in and he'll be as calm as ever. Quite the opposite of me, actually.

But I remember very vividly the pain I felt in my heart. My first born. Literally flown the nest. You could say.

A few weeks later we are visiting my parents.

"Now you know how we felt when you all went off to boarding school," my dad commiserates when I tell him how I felt. My mom, Princess Eunice Bosede (She's the daughter of a Nigerian king actually and we better not forget it), looks on sympathetically.

"Really?"

Considering all the stress we went through at boarding school back then, I would have been more than happy to be what we called a day student and attend school daily from home.

Your child could fly the nest actually at any stage of their lives. At eleven to go to boarding school, at sixteen to go on to sixth form somewhere far away – like 6000 miles. It may be university, then they may decide to move out and live on their own or with friends or they may get married. Ouch!

For each child the timing may be different, but the feeling is the same. Your little boy or girl is growing or grown up, and is not that dependent on you anymore. A hard morsel to swallow but the truth anyway.

Whatever their age you must begin to prepare yourself to let go. And you feel it happening little by little as the months and years go by.

For instance your son is getting dressed ready to go out and you are too. Since dad has taken the car you ask, "Are you going out? I'll walk with you to the bus station."

"Err...... mom, you won't be able to walk as fast as me. You take your time. I'll get a move on".

Never mind, that it's only 5-7 minutes walk. You get the message.

What your 19 year old is really saying is , "You know I love you, mom, but I don't want my friends seeing me walk into the bus station with my mother. I'll look like a mummy's boy".

You know that's kind of true especially when you unconsciously reach out to try and hold his hand when you are about to cross the road.

Back at home in the evening he tells you, "Mom, I saw you plodding along and hurrying into the bus station from the top of the bus 79."

"Yeah, I bet you were hoping I'd miss it and have to wait for another", I retort. "Never mind, I wasn't going to come up and sit with you anyway!"

You catch a little grimace and look of regret on his face. Did it seem to hurt a little? Probably. But it's only natural. Your mom and dad went through the same stage with you too. Now it's your turn.

If they never went to Boarding school as a child or teenager, you feel it the more when they go off to Uni. While you are dying inside, they are so excited to at last be getting away from home. Ouch! Again.

I was talking to my younger brother, Femi, at a family wedding in London recently. Their first child – Tunmise - a son - was getting ready to move up to Liverpool also in England, to attend university there. I asked after his daughter, Zoe and my sister in law, Tiwa.

"Get yourself ready because she's going to cry when he leaves" I say.

"She's been crying already" he replies. "And he doesn't leave until 2 weeks".

My heart goes out to her. For 18 years you see him almost every day, except for school trips and now you're not going to see him for weeks. It hurts. A lot.

As a parent you are happy that they are getting on with life and their studies but you can't help but feel a deep sadness, that they are leaving home.

Oh well, you can take solace in the sweet fact that the Universities kick them out of their accommodation in the June of every year and they have to come home anyway.

For 3 months!!

Hurray!!

You start counting the days right after they leave.

And so it is year after year. They are in and out of the house. For short periods. Sometimes for long periods of time. And if you are truly blessed, they love coming back. The older they get, the more sensitive we hope they become. Appreciating your love and the sacrifices you made for them. Helping out in the house, trying to show you that they do love you. Flying out and flying back in. In, out, in, out.

Until they fall in love.

Always on the phone

If your child has been at home for most of his or her life, going to boarding school, university but coming back for weeks or months on end for holiday, get ready for the final departure. Getting married.

You see the signs when they are always on the phone – for hours on end. Going about the house with some silly grin on their faces and having their beloved's picture on the phone, their desktop, under their pillow, in their Bible – you name it.

They never used to bother about answering the house phone before. The phone rings and rings and you yell from wherever you are, "Can somebody please get that phone!!". There'll be some loud argument amongst them on who picked it up last and hopefully before the caller hangs up, one of them reluctantly answers the call.

Not any more. Unless they have a working mobile phone in hand and that means unless they have credit on their phone, as soon as the phone rings they rush for it like a rocket.

But if they do have credit on their mobile phones, it's hours and hours up in their bedroom. No TV. No football games. Just talk, talk, talk on the phone. Those are the signs. Watch out for them.

Although sometimes it can hit you like a bomb too. Unexpectedly.

Like it was with Rebekkah.

Getting Married

Rebekkah's leaving!!

"Just that morning she was up early getting ready to go out and do her morning chores. A lovely girl she was. Never gave us much trouble. Never mixed up with bad friends. She was very kind and hospitable too. And we really loved her. She was just about reaching the age of consent to be married, but we didn't think much about that. She still had many months to go before we began to feel apprehensive about it. Many more months to go.

How wrong we were.

Just this morning she was our little girl, our sweet little baby girl.

But by night fall, she wasn't solely ours anymore. She was being whisked off to marry a good kind man, right before our very eyes.

I'd heard the story of Abram and Sarai as soon as I could understand it. They had moved on from where we all lived in UR of the Chaldees to an unknown place, or least that's what Abram had told us. He said God had told him to leave his entire clan behind and make his home some where else. No one knew where they were going but the family hoped they'd keep in touch.

And they had, from time to time. And one blessed morning we received news from the travelling traders that Sarah, (she had changed her name by then) had at last given birth to a baby boy, after so many years of unfruitfulness. Isaac he was called. We were pleased for them, but didn't think too much about it for a long time. They lived so far away anyway.

Until this morning, when all of a sudden a tall stranger came with news from them, that Isaac was looking for a wife! And where do you think he came looking ? Right on our street. And who do you think the LORD Jehovah had chosen for him? Our own dear Rebekkah!

My heart is bleeding. He stayed the night and wanted to return as soon as possible and Rebekkah also wanted to go with him. Can you imagine that? Rebekkah's not even looking back. She's eager to go and get married. My heart is bleeding. My little girl is leaving."

When you read about the union between Rebekkah and Isaac in the Big book [2] you wonder what it will feel like when your child finally flies out of your nest to get married.

The experience can bring a nostalgia of mixed feelings. Joy that at last your little girl is now a fully grown woman preparing to become a wife and hopefully will soon be a mummy herself. You have done well with God helping you and you can sit back and relax from all the labours of the past 20 something years.

Or it could be your little boy taking a wife. You are proud. You've tried your best to bring him up well and he hasn't disappointed you. Yes you are happy.

But deep down inside you are sad too. You are gaining a new son or daughter but it will never be the same again. You have to take the back seat in the driving car of your child's life now. You are no longer the driving force. You are no longer his main love. She loves someone else now with a much greater and deeper passion. And it seems like that person has taken your place. And rightfully too. That person is first now. You are second and as the children start coming, you become third place , fourth, fifth, depending on how many. Never quite first place again.

And if his nose needs wiping, it's not going to be you doing it now. Wasn't that the same with you when you got married? Now you know how it feels.

But do you know if all goes to plan and you play your cards right (with God, of course), instead of losing a child, you might be getting double what you had before.

A brand new daughter to love and cherish and to be loved by. Just like we were given.

Olubunmi Amope.[3]

Much awaited first daughter. A gift from God. Beautifully and wonderfully crafted.

And so much loved.

Chapter Eighteen

When It Doesn't Work Out the Way You Hoped It Would

What do you do when all the dreams and aspirations you have had for your child all turns sour?

What do you do when despite all you have tried to do for your child, it turns out to be fruitless?

What do you do when your child "falls by the wayside", gets caught up in gang culture, or drugs, drink or promiscuity?

Is there a time to cut yourself off from your child?

What do you do when you are so filled with shame and your heart is breaking?

What do you do when all hope seems to be lost?

When it hasn't worked out the way it should what can you do?

The Big Book tells the story about a man who found himself in just that predicament. He was wealthy and had 2 sons to whom he was preparing to leave his fortune to when he died. His older son was a good, respectful and reliable boy. A joy to any parent's heart. Hardworking and well balanced. The second son? A real parent's heart breaker you may say.

We are not told of how his childhood or teenage years transpired but as soon as he was old enough he demanded his inheritance from his father and hit the road...probably never intending to come back.

Why did his dad let him have his inheritance? I cannot tell. Maybe he was such a pain in the house that it was the best thing to do to let him go. Or maybe he needed to learn about life the hard way . . . not wanting to learn the easy way from his dad and his mom.

Whatever the reason, he collected his inheritance from his father and left home.

As the story unfolds we see what kind of person he was. He loved the booze and the women. He must have thought to himself, "Yes! I'm free from their nagging and lecturing. I can do what ever I want now".

And he did just that.

He spent all his money on wild friends, partying and riotous living - never thinking of saving, investing or multiplying what he had received. He wasted it all. Every single penny. Until he had nothing left.

He then began to learn the lesson his parents had probably been trying to teach him all his life. He began to suffer. No friends. No shelter. No money. No food. Nothing.

He found a job keeping pigs but even the pigs food was not given to him to eat. The Big Book refers to him as the prodigal son.[1]

In another chapter it also tells the story of another bad son.

Did I say bad?

Actually he was even worse.

He was the son of a great king, the greatest king in the history of that land. But he was a cunning conniving evil prince. If he had asked for his inheritance from his father that would also have been wrong but understandable but no, what does he do? He wants the kingdom, even while his dad is still alive and so he woos the people and turns their hearts away from his father and over to himself. He plans a coup and tries to topple his dad from off the throne.

He almost succeeds but the God of his father, David, did not allow it. Unlike the young man in the earlier story, who eventually came back home begging his dad's forgiveness, Absalom was not so lucky. He lost his life in the process.[2]

When the Creator God, made man he gave him a very special ability – He gave him the option of choice. So we see the first man and woman to be created on earth, having the ability to choose to obey God or not to. And we all since then have been given that same ability. To obey God and do good or to disobey God or do what is wrong or what does not please Him.

In one of the chapters of the Book, we see God speaking about 2 little boys even while they were still in their mother's womb.

"I love one of them," He declares, "but I hate the other".[3]

Strange, even when neither of them had been born, God know that one of them will exercise his option to do what is wrong instead of what is right. God is almost saying, "There's nothing I can do about it. He will make up his mind to do what is wrong. It's his choice. I cannot change it. I can plead with him. I can cajole him. I can beg him. But I cannot force him. I have given him the option to choose. I will not take that away from him".

Awesome. Isn't it? But the naked truth. We all have a choice to do what is right or to do what is wrong. Our children have that choice also. We can steer them, teach them, instruct them, pray for them and lead them along the right path. In most cases especially when we start on time, when they are still very small and malleable, they will follow the right path.

But sometimes due to many reasons, due to no fault of the parents some children may not.

I have said this is due to many factors. Some children are victims of the environment they were born and brought up in and so they turn out bad. But yet some children are born with a silver spoon in the mouths, sent to the best schools, never lacked for anything good and yet they still turned out bad.

Sometimes, we start out too late to effectively monitor or discipline our children. We are unaware of the forces and influences around them that are waiting to destroy their destinies and devour their souls.

Right from when a child is born, the Enemy is looking out to see if He can subtly draw them over to his side and wreck their lives.

Do you have an Enemy? Oh yes, you do! We all do! If you are a Christian, you must be aware of this from day one. If you are not, you can only use physical methods, the effective spiritual methods that bring permanent results will sadly be out of your reach.

The Big Book helps us with tips and advice on how to ensure we protect our children from the influences of the Enemy and how to make sure they grow up to be well adjusted men and women in the society. And hopefully we will start before it's too late. We'll discuss this when we get to the chapter that talks about Your Faith.

But back to the reality that sometimes it does seem like we either did start too late, or the child just seems to have chosen to follow a different path.

What can we do?

Pray and ask others to continue to pray

Never give up

A prodigal child's turn around may take years and sadly for some, may not even happen in the life time of the parent. Never give up. Be positive and believe that God will bring a turn around for you.

Seek for help when it all seems too much to bear

Never close the door irreversibly

When a child's ways are dangerous to you and the rest of the family, you may be forced to distance yourself from that child for safety reasons. For instance Pastor Sam (not his real name) had to keep his son in the boy's quarters – a back house in his compound. He provided him with shelter but didn't allow him to have access to the main house because the son would steal the family property and sell it to fuel his habit of drug addiction. But never close that door irreversibly. Let your child know you will always be there for them as much as it lies in your power and strength to be.

As long as we live we will constantly be looking out for the welfare of our children, for even in adulthood there still remains tendency to go astray.

I read a story a long time ago about 2 adult children who turned from a good and perfect existence into one that brought them pain and sorrow and almost broke the heart of their Father.

They started out well, this man and his wife.

They were so much in love. Not a care in the world. The man so perfectly loved, the woman safe, secure and submissive in his love.

They had all they needed. Well formed, well educated, perfectly knowledgeable, the perfect couple. Just made for each other – you could say.

The woman perfectly groomed, not a hair out of place, a figure to die for. The man – six pack, tall and strong. The perfect man.

They lived in the best home. Beautiful. The lighting, the decoration, the heating – just perfect. It was never too cold and never too hot.

And the food! Delicious! As beautiful as the woman was she was also the best cook for miles around. Her food was like the food of heaven. After eating her food you wouldn't want to eat from anywhere else again.

And to crown it all, they had this Godfather. A Mentor. Someone always looking out for them. Someone they could run to for help if they ever needed it. He was always at their beck and call. Always there for them. He invested a great deal of Himself into them for He loved them dearly.

They had what you and I would describe as the perfect life.

But alas, what could and should have lasted years and years , suddenly came to an abrupt end.

The woman became restless. She had all she wanted. She had all she needed. But after a while it seemed all that was still not enough. She became restless. "Surely there's more to life than this", she reminisced. "Surely I can have even more. Surely this is not all there is".

Maybe she discussed her feelings with her husband, maybe she didn't, I cannot tell. The story does not say. But her restlessness, her insatiable appetite opened her to the attack of their Enemy. He had always been waiting for an opportunity, for he hated their God father and vowed to destroy anything or anyone that was precious to him. And so he had been waiting. She didn't even know he was lurking around her, waiting to steal, kill and destroy her life . [4]

And so when she was at her lowest point, he subtly moved in, offering her an alternative kind of lifestyle, a different type of existence, different from what she was used to but pleasing to her insatiability.

"You don't need to remain the way you are", He hisses. "I can introduce you to something so much better. I can give you pleasures, powers, riches that are so much more fulfilling than what you have now.

And he dangled the deception that brings destruction, before her eyes. She could be her own master, chart her own destiny. No one would tell her what to do, how to live.

"I 'll make my own rules, behave the way I want," she muses. " I 'll take no advice from anybody. I'll be my own god."

If you know the ancient writings you would recognise by now, who I am taking about. She swallowed the lie, hook, line and sinker. She ate the forbidden piece and was initiated into the "promised" better existence. But alas! Was it better?

She immediately felt different. She was no longer the same. Her perfection was gone. A bad thought skipped through her mind. She'd never thought evil before. Did she feel a little bit tired, all of a sudden? She'd never been tired in her entire life. There was a bitter taste in her mouth but she brushed it off, pushing the feeling of alarm to the back of her mind. "When my love comes home, I'll feel better".

As soon as he does return from work, she feeds her husband the lie. As her looks at her, he knows her nature has changed, but because of the love he has for her, he receives the deception into his soul and they both fall thousands of miles from their elevated position to the depths of hell.

After that first step of self defiance, disloyalty and rebellion, everything changes. Sin is introduced into their lives. Their love is no longer perfect. They begin to accuse each other. "It's your fault", he says.

"No, it's the Enemy that made me do it" she replies.

Surely and truly, they lose everything. They begin to age, get sick, toil for their food. They lose their home, their love, their future and saddest of all - they lose the help, cover, protection and intimacy of the God Father. Even He cannot reverse the implications of their deed. They now belong to the Enemy as they have chosen to obey him and be initiated into his domain. He is now their master and they have taken on his nature to themselves. They must do what he commands now and his commandments are grievous. He takes over their homes, their hearts, their lives and their souls.

One act of disobedience, one act of sin, one act of rebellion – has far reaching effects that are so terrible and so irreversible. Even the God father, the ever present Help - cannot help them now!

Or can He?

The ancient landmarks, the written and spoken words that keep the world in place cannot be broken. The soul that sins, shall die [5]; It's been written. It's been established. It cannot be changed. It's settled forever and ever.[6]

But the God father is wise and nothing takes Him by surprise. There is a secret Person, very close to Him that nobody knew existed. He has a Son!!

No one knows of His existence – at least not in the realm of Adam and Eve, for that was the name of the man and his wife. Even the Enemy, the destroyer, the devil, Satan the once trusted right hand man of the God father was not aware of His capabilities.

That He could change His form – Be God and yet become a foetus, a baby in the womb of a woman, be born and grow to become a man, just like you!!

And so after years and years and thousands of years of suffering, pain, sickness and death, the God father plays His joker Card – His Son, Jesus is introduced into the world, to reverse the effects of sin that Adam and Eve allowed to enter in, so many eons ago.

He was born of a woman [7] like we were.

He had skin, blood and bones – like we have.

He was tempted by the devil – like His ancestors Adam and Eve were and like we were too. But – He did not sin [8]

135

He was baptised with the Holy Spirit [9] just like the apostles were at Pentecost[10] and like we have been ever since.

He lived like a man, prayed like a man, wept like a man, was hungry like a man. He loved like a man, had compassion like a man and eventually did for us what no man could do for us – dying an innocent man on a wooden cross.[11]

He was sinless , shedding His blood for the remission of our sins and reversing the curse of death that was upon our lives.[12]

All we have to do is to acknowledge His visitation, for even now He still visits us, knocking at the door of our hearts.[13]

He wants to be born in us again today as He was years ago in that stable in Bethlehem, where he was first born. He wants so dearly for us to attain that perfect state of sons and daughters of the God father, living forever and ever with Him in a glorious existence.

Are you hurting over a prodigal child? Put all your trust in this God Father. He loves your child much more than you ever can. When it gets to the stage that you can do no more on your own, you may just have to leave it in His hands.

And trust Him.

Shalom.

Epilogue

*I*s it all over?

The Big Book talks about times and seasons.

It says, there is a time and a season for everything under heaven[1]. In heaven there is no passage of time. It'll be one glorious wonderful existence but here on earth we are led, driven and controlled by time.

There is a time for childhood. There is a time for youth. There is a time for maturity. There is a time for middle age and one day hopefully by God's grace there'll be a time when we will grow old.

We all bow to the passing of time. No man can avoid it not matter how he tries. No matter how much money you have acquired. No matter how much plastic surgery you can afford to do to try and slow it down. Time passes for us all.

And one day your little son or daughter, your teenager who you love so much and have invested so much of this precious time into, will grow up and leave home. Time is moving for them too and soon they will be where you were. Graduating from University. Starting a job or business endeavour. Getting married. Having children. Moving on with time. Moving on with their own life.

When this comes to pass, you may be blessed to have a spouse who is still around you and with whom you can grow old together. Or you may be alone. Sometimes life gives us what we didn't really expect.

But whatever your circumstance may be there is Someone who will never ever leave you.

The Big Book says He has loved you from the beginning, forming you by Himself in His own image, in His likeness. No matter how dissatisfied you may be with your looks or body structure, you actually look like Him and He loves you just the way you are.

He was there at the very beginning, when your mother pushed you out of her own womb. Even long before that - right at the moment of your conception He was there showering you with love and making sure that you were perfectly formed and protected through the changing trimesters of pregnancy.

He has written a long letter to you in the big Book called the Bible and in it He promises to never leave you nor forsake you. I am with you always He promises, even until time comes to an end.

You may be a Christian as you read this book or you may not be. It's not a matter of religion my friend. It's a matter of life and death. And that Life is a Person. That Life is a Man. That Life is a Man who is also God.

Very strange to believe. In fact that is what we call a mystery. That God Almighty, the Creator of the heavens and the earth, could manifest in a different form as a person like you and me. "And why would He do that?" you may rightfully ask.

Because time passes and we will not be here forever. But there is somewhere else that we can go to. Somewhere much better and much more wonderfully fulfilling than where we are now. Somewhere where there is no growing old or painful separations or departures. A blissful experience that will last forever. But you have to be made ready to go there. You have to learn about how to get there and Someone has to give you a ticket to make that journey. And that person must be Someone who has paid the price and has gone ahead to make room for you when you arrive.

You may have heard of Him before or you may not have. His name is Jesus Christ. The Saviour of the world. The One who loves you with an everlasting love. The One who is waiting to get to know you. The One who will help you bring up your child in a way that when he/she is grown, will be a delight to you, your family and the world at large. And the One who will be with you always even when it's time for them to leave. He invites you to come to Him for a relationship that will never ever come to an end.

And when you do get to know Him (as I hope you will) you'll realise that it is not over at all. In fact life is only just beginning. And when the time comes when you do eventually step out of this world, you'll just step into another. I will too and one day I'll see you there!!!

Why not take up His invitation now?

Shalom.

Bibliography

My Son, My daughter – Prologue

Chapter 1

Needs and Wants
1. The Big Book is the Bible.
2. Solomon was the son of David, King of Israel who succeeded him as king of the United Kingdom. The kingdom became divided into two during the reign of his son, Rehoboam.
3. 1st Kings 11:3;
4. Ecclesiastes 1:2;
5. 2nd Chronicles 10:16;
6. Philippians 4:19;
7. Psalm 37:4;

Chapter 2

Just Because We Liked It Yesterday...

1. Asda Stores Limited is a British supermarket chain which retails food, clothing, general merchandise, toys and financial services.

Chapter 3

Sibling Rivalry

1. Genesis 25:26;

2. The Bar Mitzvah is the Jewish coming of age ceremony for boys. It normally took place when a boy was about 13 years old.

3. Genesis 25:29-33;

4. Genesis 27:1-4;

5. Genesis 25 – 28;

Chapter 4

To Smack or Not to Smack

1. Proverbs 23:13;

2. Romans 5:13;

3. Proverbs 22:6;

4. Culled from Mail Online by Daniel Martin 30th January 2012. Boris Johnson has backed calls for parents to be allowed to smack their children to instil discipline.

The Mayor of London spoke after a senior Labour MP blamed his party's partial ban on smacking children for last August's riots.

Former education minister David Lammy called for a return to Victorian laws on discipline, saying working-class parents needed to be able to use corporal punishment to deter unruly children from joining gangs and wielding knives.

He claimed parents were 'no longer sovereign in their own homes' and feared that social workers would take their children away if they chastised them.

Labour's 2004 law did not completely ban smacking, but said a smack should cause no more than a reddening of the skin.

Last night Mr Johnson supported Mr Lammy, saying the current law was 'confusing', meaning that parents do not know how far they can go in terms of smacking their children.

'People do feel anxious about imposing discipline on their children, whether the law will support them,' he told the Pienaar's Politics programme on BBC Radio 5 Live.

'I think there ought to be some confirmation that the benefit of the doubt will always be given to parents in these matters and they should be seen as the natural figures of authority in this respect.

'I think there ought to be some confirmation that the benefit of the doubt will always be given to parents in these matters and they should be seen as the natural figures of authority in this respect'

'Obviously you don't want to have a licence for physical abuse or for violence and that's very important.'

The Mayor said he believed he had the support of Education Secretary Michael Gove.

'I know that people will have their own views, but let me just say on the issue that's been raised a lot of times with me; the issue of are you allowed to chastise, are you allowed to impose discipline?'

Chapter 5

No! You Can't!

1. Matthew 7:7;
2. short for University
3. second year in high school. Students aged from 12 years of age
4. Genesis 34:1-end
5. Hebrews 4:15;

Chapter 6

The Room, The Bed and All Those Clothes on the Floor

    1. Author unknown

Chapter 7

Their Relationships

    1. Ephesians 2:19;

Chapter 8

What on Earth Do You Think You Are Wearing?

    1. Ecclesiastes 1:9;

    2. Hebrews 13:8;

    3. 1st Peter 2:9;

Chapter 9

When One Seems Smarter than the Other

    1. 2nd Corinthians 10:12;

    2. Psalm 139:4;

Chapter 10

Express Your Love

    1. Song of Solomon

    2. John 3:16

Chapter 11

Making Sweet Memories

1. Southfork Ranch is a conference and event center located in Parker, Texas, U.S., about 25 mi (40 km) north of Dallas; it contains the Ewing Mansion, where the Ewing family lived in the TV series Dallas.

Chapter 12

Let the Little Children Come to Me and ...Talk

Chapter 13

Sow a Good Seed, Reap a Good Harvest

1. Proverbs 24:16;
2. Ecclesiastes 7:9;

Chapter 14

Your Faith

1. John 3:16;

Chapter 15

Your Time

Chapter 16

Do You Have to Talk About Sex?

1. 2nd Samuel 13:1-8;

Chapter 17

Flying the Nest

1. The Republic du Benin is the next country to the west of Nigeria.

2. Genesis 24

3. Our first daughter in law, married to our first son, Tosho.

Chapter 18

When it Doesn't Work Out the Way You Hoped it Would.

1. Luke 15:13-31;

2. 2nd Samuel 13,14;

3. Romans 9:13;

4. John 10:10;

5. Romans 6:23;

6. Psalm 119:89;

7. Matthew 1:21;

8. Matthew 4:1-11;

9. Luke 3:21-22;

10. Acts 2:1-4

11. Hebrews 4:15;

12. Matthew 26:28;

13. Revelation 3:20;

Chapter 19

Is it all over? – Epilogue

1. Ecclesiastes 3:1;